REMEMBERING WORLD WAR II IN THE PHILIPPINES

VOLUME 2

NATIONAL HISTORICAL COMMISSION
OF THE PHILIPPINES

Published by:

NATIONAL HISTORICAL COMMISSION OF THE PHILIPPINES
T.M. Kalaw St., Ermita
Manila, Philippines
Tel. 5335-1212 · www.nhcp.gov.ph

Recommended entry:

Remembering World War II in the Philippines:
    Volume II, Manila : National Historical Commission
    of the Philippines, c2022.
        pp. ; cm.

1.   World War II -- Philippines   I. Title

ISBN: 978-971-538-207-6
Reprint 2022

Cover photos courtesy of Dr. Ricardo T. Jose

Foreword

The National Historical Institute, now the National Historical Commission of the Philippines (NHCP), commemorated the 60ᵗʰ anniversary of the end of World War II through a series of activities that included two conferences on the Japanese occupation of the Philippines and the resistance to it. Both historians and people who survived the war served as resource speakers during these February and August 2005 conferences.

The NHCP is pleased to release the second volume of these proceedings for the symposium held at the Graduate School of the University of Santo Tomas from 16–17 August 2005. Like the first volume published in 2007, this compilation presents stories of civilians, Filipinos and foreigners alike, during the years when the country was under Japanese rule. Narrated by a diverse group of people, and includes that of an American Jesuit priest who was detained with fellow ecclesiastics at San Agustin Church and the Los Baños internee camp; a business tycoon's ordeal when he, along with his family, trekked through the cold highlands of North Luzon to escape the carpet bombing of Baguio; a respected artist raging against the takeover of a sovereign nation; an academic's candid depiction of the petty rivalries of some guerrillas. Information on various battle strategies used by the Allies and guerrilla forces, and the collaboration issue which never had a formal and just closure are likewise included in this volume.

The NHCP hopes that this volume will provide readers valuable insights six decades after the war and that this part of our history will not occur again.

National Historical Commission of the Philippines

Contents

Keynote Address at the Conference on "World War II in the Philippines, 60 Years After," Manila, 16–17 August 2005

Fr. Miguel Bernad, S.J.

This year of 2005 marks the 60th anniversary of the end of the Second World War, the most terrible war in human history. The end of that war was, therefore, an event of tremendous significance, and its 60th anniversary is being celebrated in many places. In the Philippines, there is no celebration. There is instead something much more useful, namely this Conference that we are having, a serious attempt to promote scholarly reflection on the various aspects and consequences of that war as it

1

affected our country. For organizing this Conference, the National Historical Institute deserves great credit.

Few events in human history have been so devastating as the Second World War. Its toll on human lives was in the hundreds of millions. Unlike the wars of previous centuries, the casualties of World War II were not only soldiers. A very large proportion were civilians. And that is one of the most important aspects of that war.

Shakespeare's Othello could speak glowingly of what he called "glorious war." His farewell to war is one of the more famous passages of that play:

> Farewell the plumed troop, and the big wars
> That made ambition virtue...
> Farewell the neighing steed, and the shrill trump,
> The spirit-stirring drum, the ear-piercing fife,
> The royal banner, and all quality
> Pride, pomp and circumstance of glorious war!
>
> — Othello III

That was in the old days when war was colorful, when only soldiers were involved in the fighting, when French knights demanded the exclusive right to fight in the front lines, with the British relegated merely to the rear. Civilians were not involved, except when unruly troops came in and sacked their cities. World War One and particularly World War Two changed the very nature of war. These were world wars in the most ghastly realistic sense of the word. They were total wars where everyone in the nation was involved and there were no front lines. The result was the destruction of cities: Warsaw in Poland, Dresden in Germany, Coventry and parts of London in England. And in the Philippines, Cebu, Zamboanga, Cagayan de Misamis, and, of course, Manila.

Most terrifying of all, Hiroshima. Hiroshima began a new age in warfare. It made us aware of the possibility that one nuclear blast could destroy an entire civilization.

It was not just the physical destruction of cities and buildings. It was the irreparable loss of much of the cultural heritage of the world. One of the many buildings destroyed in World War II was Montecasino in Italy, perhaps the most famous and the most historic of monasteries, founded by St. Benedict. After the war, an American weekly magazine published a remark by an American soldier. Did he say, Why the fuss about the destruction of a monastery? It was an old building and two million dollars can build a much better one.

I remember Father Leo Cullum, himself a very loyal American, saying to me, "What a stupid remark of that soldier. No amount of dollars could possibly replace Montecasino."

If the Taj Mahal were to be destroyed, or Angkor Wat, or Borubudur, or any of the great cathedrals, no amount of dollars or euros or yens could possibly replace them. One madman with a hammer had tried to destroy Michaelangelo's *Pieta*. Fortunately he succeeded in destroying only the Virgin's fingers. Had the entire statue been destroyed, the loss would have been irreparable.

Which brings us to our own country.

Rizal in 1896 spoke about his death as a sleep in an enchanted land. *Y en tu encantada tierra la eternidad dormir*. Some years later Fernando Maria Guerrero described the Philippines as a bower of beautiful flowers:

> *Pilipinas es un nido*
> *formado de hermosas flores.*

He was not speaking merely of the countryside. He also meant the Manila that he knew and its *arrabales*. He lived in Ermita and walked everyday to school, past Bagumbayan Field into the Walled City to the Ateneo, which was then on Arzobispo Street.

Some decades later I lived in Ermita, at the Ateneo on Padre Faura Street. Occasionally I followed the same route that Fernando Maria Guerrero took, through the streets of Ermita, across the Luneta, to Intramuros. Intramuros was still intact: its walls, its gates, its buildings and cobbled streets. The buildings had become a little shabby, but the churches were magnificent. And especially that gem of baroque art, the church of San Ignacio, with its carved ceiling, its grooved pillars, its ornate pulpit, all of the hardwood carved on the spot by Filipino craftsmen. It is said that in 1903 the government wanted to dismantle San Ignacio church and bring it across the ocean to set it up in the St. Louis Exposition as a supreme example of Philippine Art.

If Intramuros had become a little shabby, Ermita and Malate had not. These were spruce, clean, well-maintained residential districts, with tree-lined streets, sidewalks, and modest but neat houses fronting them. One particular street was especially beautiful, Isaac Peral (now renamed United National Avenue) a wide street with tall over-arching trees, and with fine buildings along with it, including the elegant Episcopalian church of St. Mary and St. John. The Ateneo in Ermita had two towers. I used to go up to the western tower that commanded a view of Manila Bay, and the mountains of Cavite and Bataan beyond. But if one looked down from that tower on Ermita, one saw the tops of trees, for Manila was a beautiful city that gloried in its trees.

Beyond Ermita and beyond the Luneta was the Palace of the Legislature, designed in neo-classical style by Juan Arellano. In the basement was the National Library, with its valuable collection of Filipiniana that had formerly belonged to the Tabacalera in Barcelona. Also in the basement was the National Museum, with Rizal's manuscripts in glass cases. It was there that I saw the *garrote vil*, which had strangled the three priests, Burgos, Gomes, and Zamora.

After the war, all that was a heap of rubble— Intramuros, the Legislative Building, Ermita, Malate. Of the Filipiniana collection that had belonged to the Tabacalera, all that was left (as one Spanish writer has remarked) was the magnificent three volume catalogue compiled by Retana.

There was one survivor in Intramuros: the Augustinian church. But the priory was destroyed, including the 300-year old library.

And the friars? The friars were among the thousands in Manila massacred by the Japanese.

Genocide is a newly coined word. But its reality began during World War II with the systematic attempt to exterminate the Jewish race.

The word genocide has not been applied to the killings in Manila and the provinces. But what also do you call a deliberate, long-planned attempt to kill as many human beings as possible—men, women, children—in Manila, in Laguna, in Batangas, and other places?

Father Haggerty in his book says that from the hills in Bukidnon he watched the American bombers drop their bombs on Cagayan de Oro (at the time called Cagayan de Misamis). They demolished the cathedral, the *convento*, the bishop's house, the Ateneo de Cagayan, and many other buildings. In fifteen minutes (says Father Haggerty) the bombers had destroyed the work of years.

Zamboanga used to be a beautiful city. The old song proudly proclaimed its beauty.

Zamboanga la bella, Hermosa, gentil,
orgullo de Mindanao

They still sing that song, but it has become meaningless, for Zamboanga, demolished by the war, has lost its beauty.

In Cebu the Jesuits founded a little school in 1595 and called it Colegio de San Ildefonso. It grew to be a large institution, with a fine three-storey building of stone and a church beside it. In 1768 when the Jesuits were expelled from all Spanish possessions, the Crown took over the college and (like all the Jesuit colleges in Spain and the Spanish colonies) renamed it San Carlos in honor of the patron saint of King Carlos III. All that, with much of Cebu, was still standing in 1944. In 1945 all that was nothing but rubble.

Besides the physical destruction of lives and structures was the destruction of a culture. The Philippines that emerged from the rubble in 1945 was not the same as the one before the war in 1941. A whole social order and a way of life died during the Japanese occupation.

When families that lived in opulence before the war had to go begging afterwards, things were not the same.

Before the war, a Justice of the Supreme Court, one of the most learned and one of the most respected, resigned from the bench—not because of anything wrong he had done, but because a niece had been accused of wrongdoing. That bespoke an exquisite feeling of *delicadeza*. How many people would do that today?

In 1942, during the Japanese Occupation, I watched from a third floor window of the Observatory wing of the Ateneo on Padre Faura Street in Ermita. Directly across from my window was the small three-storey building of the Commission on National Language, dwarfed by the much larger buildings of the University of the Philippines. The Japanese soldiers has just taken possession of the building and they were preparing it for their habitation. They threw everything out of the window: first books, then manuscripts, and papers of all kinds. Then typewriters came flying out the window and landed on the ground with a clang. Below in the yard, a soldier with a rake was raking up all the books and papers into a large pile and set the whole thing on fire. Valuable books perhaps, and manuscripts, the work of years of labor by Filipino scholars went up in smoke. Then from out the window came all the wooden furniture: chairs, desks, empty bookshelves. These were cut up into small pieces for firewood.

Those were the simple needs of the soldiers: an empty floor space to sleep on, and plenty of firewood with which to cook their meals. Those are the elemental values of war, the values of an ignorant conquering army that had no respect for the cultural heritage of a conquered people.

But all is not lost. Some good things have survived the war, and some good things have resulted from it. Like all wars, this one brought out the worst and the best in people. There were scoundrels and traitors. And there were heroes.

People who evacuated from the cities and towns and lived in the rural areas discovered that normal life could be maintained without any imported goods.

This was particularly the case in Mindanao, where only the coastal towns were held by the Japanese, and the majority of the people had moved to the hinterland. I asked them if the war had brought any benefits. "Yes," they said, They mentioned a few. People learned to live simply, using only the resources available locally. They learned to improvise. They also learned skills. One lady said she had learned to make children's dresses out of *retazos*. These were traded for foodstuffs with the Subanons and other tribal people in the hills. The mountain people liked the cotton dresses because they were softer and lighter than the heavy cloth that they themselves wove from abaca hemp.

More important (they said) families were brought closer together. Members of the family walked together, worked together, helped each other.

There was also one totally unexpected result. There had been much anti-clericalism before the war, much disparaging of the Catholic Church, an attitude learned from the teachers from across the ocean. The war (like all adversity) made people realize how much they depended on God, and how much they needed the priest and it brought them closer to their priests. In Mindanao, missionaries of various nationalities were kept safe from the Japanese because people risked their lives to protect them.

This goes to show that the old Spanish proverb still holds: *No hay mal que por bien no venga.* There is no evil that does not result in some good.

The Plans to Defend Luzon, 1941 and 1944

Jose Antonio Custodio

INTRODUCTION

Sixty years after the end of the Second World War, many misconceptions remain about the defense of the Philippines by the USAFFE in 1941–1942 and the Japanese in 1944–1945. Many believe that in 1941 there was no hope of victory for the USAFFE and that in 1945, Yamashita's strategy was correct or that he had no involvement in the Battle for Manila. This paper intends to clear up many of these misconceptions most of which were brought about by historical prejudices.

THE AMERICAN DEFENSE PLAN 1941–1942

In April 1941 War Plan ORANGE-3 (WPO-3), was completed. The color orange was used to identify plans in the event of a war between the United States and

Japan. The plan assumed a surprise attack with less than 48 hours warning if at all, by the Japanese against U.S. and allied forces and called for the Philippine garrison to hold out until the arrival of reinforcements. It was believed that the Japanese would deploy approximately 100,000 men to invade the Philippines for the purpose of severing U.S. lines of communication in Asia. It was also believed that Luzon with its fine harbor in Manila would be the site of the major attack of the Japanese.

Thus, the Initial Protective Force as the Philippine garrison was called in the plan had the primary mission of protecting Manila Bay and denying it to the enemy. In order to defend Manila Bay, it was crucial to hold out in Bataan because it overlooked Manila. Furthermore, the islands at the mouth of the bay were fortified to add to the defenses. The six year old Philippine Army was to provide considerable additional reinforcement to the initial U.S. forces (namely the Philippine Division) already deployed. It was estimated that the garrison could hold out for six months. The Philippine Division commander was tasked with organizing the defenses of Bataan. There was to be modest air and naval support assisting in the defense of the Philippines.

It was estimated that a force of 40,000 men was sufficient to hold out in Bataan for 180 days. The bulk of the supplies were at Manila and there had to be sufficient time provided by the rearguard for these items to be brought over to Bataan. The civilian sector was also tapped to provide additional transport for the supplies to be brought into Bataan. This assessment turned out to be overly optimistic since it did not take into consideration advances in military technology, the aggressive tactics of the Japanese and what is called the fog of the war which is the confusion of battle and its effect on the conduct of operations.

WPO-3 only thought of success and nothing else. It did not factor in defeat or even the probability of the U.S. Navy not sending the fleet to support the garrison. Ironically the attack on Pearl Harbor and the loss of a considerable portion of the Far East Air Force (FEAF) had the effect of psychologically shocking the U.S. Navy into inaction about the Philippines. Surprisingly, the U.S. Navy did not think that WPO-3 would succeed and were more conservative about their ability to fight their way across the Pacific to relieve the Philippine garrison.

THE REVISED DEFENSE PLAN

General Douglas MacArthur ended up coming up with a version of his plan that he hoped would nullify the inadequacies of WPO-3. His eloquence and his optimism proved the key in winning over the War Department and the rest of the U.S. government to the plan he pushed for. He came up with an aggressive plan that involved the best weapons in the U.S. arsenal then and top-caliber units that would be used, not merely to hold out passively, but to eliminate the Japanese enemy at the beaches and project power in the region. Air power was the key and he requested for the strengthening of the air component in the Philippines of which he got in November 1941. By that month, 35 B-17s and 100 modern fighters were already in the Philippines and there were more on the way. Instead of a passive garrison, MacArthur envisioned the Philippines as a self-sustaining fortress that could even block Japanese advances south. MacArthur even challenged the global military strategy of the U.S. designated Rainbow 5 which again talked about a holding out position in the Philippines and its loss to the Japanese.

MacArthur argued that by 1942, he would have a formidable force of 200,000 Filipino and American troops and modern equipment to utilize against a Japanese invasion. Had time been allotted to MacArthur, he may very well have achieved that objective of his since on the eve of the battle the United States Army Forces in the Far East (USAFFE) formed July 1941, was the most powerful American military formation outside of the U.S. and Hawaii. He was optimistic that the war could be carried to the Japanese instead of waiting for relief. Very much convinced, the U.S. government acceded to his wishes and he obtained the revision he wanted. The directives which he got from Washington were:

1. Support the Navy in raiding Japanese sea communications and destroying Axis forces.

2. Conduct air raids against Japanese forces and installations within tactical operating radius of available bases.

3. Co-operate with the Associated Powers in the defense of the territories of these Powers in accordance with approved policies and agreements.

Under MacArthur's new plan a withdrawal to Bataan was not the primary objective but the defense of the beaches was. The critical areas were Lingayen Gulf, the Zambales coast, and the Bataan peninsula, and the approach to Manila from Central Luzon. North Luzon Force commanded by General Jonathan Wainwright consisting of three PA Divisions and backed by elements of the U.S. Philippine Division would play a decisive role in containing the expected main Japanese invasion force. South Luzon Force under General George Parker guarded against an enemy landing at its area of responsibility but was weaker than NLF and therefore also much less capable. It did however have the 41st Division which was later to prove itself in Bataan.

From mid-1941 onwards, mobilization of the Philippine Army began and continued up until the Japanese invasion. More American men and equipment were pouring into the Philippines including the powerful Provisional Tank Group which had 100 M-3 light tanks that outclassed anything the Japanese had. There were also 50 self-propelled 75mm guns mounted on armored halftracks that gave a grand total of 150 armored fighting vehicles in the Philippines which was the equivalent of an armored division.

It cannot be said that MacArthur's plan was itself fanciful and unreal. Today many fault MacArthur for his order to defend the beaches. That is faulting MacArthur for the wrong thing. The plan was correct as was always proven in the Second World War that the best way to defeat an enemy is at the shoreline. Witness Dieppe, D-Day, the Leyte Landings, Okinawa and Iwo Jima. In all these battles, the enemy had to be repulsed because if not, it would be next to impossible to contain him. What doomed the Philippines was the fact that the FEAF was destroyed on the ground and this forced MacArthur to go back to the passive WPO-3 while also adding to the gloom that led to the writing off of the Philippines in 1942. Had the FEAF not been destroyed on the ground and had the USAFFE ground units enjoyed air superiority, it would have been possible that the Japanese landings in Lingayen and elsewhere would have been crushed. One must remember that the U.S. Philippine Division was a formidable force with a powerful armored complement. The FEAF could have struck back at Formosa immediately following the attack on Pearl Harbor to disrupt the Japanese aerial strike force there. It also could have provided the much needed cover for any U.S. convoy sent to re-supply the Philippines.

Success in the Philippines then would have encouraged Washington to send additional reinforcements since there was already the Pensacola convoy waiting to be sent either here or Australia. This convoy had 52 dive bombers of the 27th Bombardment Group, 18 P-40s, 340 motor vehicles, 48 75mm guns, 3,500,00 rounds of .30- and .50-caliber ammunition, 600 tons of bombs, 9,000 drums of aviation fuel, and other heavy equipment and supplies. Also aboard were the two light field artillery battalions and the ground echelon of the 7th Bombardment Group. It was never sent to the Philippines but instead was diverted to Australia though much argument to send it to the Philippines ensued before the decision to divert was given due to the already perilous situation here.

There was a great possibility that the invasion of the Philippines in 1941–42 would have been defeated by the USAFFE. One should not overestimate the Japanese who were themselves hard-pressed for units and resources. Japanese units in the Philippine invasion were stripped away by Tokyo and sent to the Dutch East Indies greatly weakening General Masaharu Homma's 14th Army. The Japanese had only sent 43,000 men who were outnumbered two to one by the USAFFE. Japanese units such as the 16th and 48th Divisions were not top-rate units. The tanks of the Japanese were outclassed by the PTG and mixes of new and old aircraft were used to provide air support to the invasion force. Furthermore, the invasion was hampered by the confusion of what was to be the objective and since Homma was ordered to capture Manila, he ignored the massive USAFFE forces pouring into Bataan. Such was the perilous state of Japanese capabilities that in February 1942 a proposal to take the offensive against the weakened 14th Army and break out of Bataan was contemplated before being set aside.

It took only several dozen planes to wipe out four Japanese fleet carriers in the Battle of Midway in June 1942 that turned the tide of the Pacific War. Had MacArthur not been affected by paralysis and so with the rest of his staff, in the first crucial hours of the war, the Philippines instead of Midway may have turned out to be the turning point of the Pacific War.

THE JAPANESE DEFENSE PLAN 1944–1945

In regard to Japanese defenses in 1944, prior to the battle for Leyte, the Japanese 14th Area Army had originally envisioned a decisive engagement with the Americans in Luzon. General Tomoyuki Yamashita was, therefore very much disturbed by the change in strategy advocated by his superiors at Imperial General Headquarters that the decisive battle would be fought at Leyte itself. General Yamashita, hence, deployed approximately 45,000 of his best troops there, including the Japanese 1st Infantry Division. What made matters worse was that many of these troops deployed to Leyte never made it there as they were destroyed en route by American air and naval power. By 19 December 1944, Leyte had been written off by General Yamashita as hopeless and the Japanese 35th Army was made to fend for itself. The effect of the Leyte campaign on the Japanese 14th Area Army strategy was that it forced them to adopt a new one that called for, at the most, delaying the enemy advance. By all intents and purposes, it was not a plan with an optimistic outlook.

THE JAPANESE PLAN TO DEFEND LUZON

At once, new plans were drawn up on how best to delay the next enemy's advance. According to a postwar account, General Yamashita's strategy aimed to take

> ...advantage of the mountains terrain, I planned to establish three strong points at Baguio and Balete Pass: the second point was west of Clark Field; the third strong point in mountains east of Manila. These plans were to carry out a delaying action.

With regards to General Yamashita's appreciation of Manila, in his trial, he stated that:

> ...First, the population of Manila is approximately one million; therefore, it is impossible to feed them. The second reason is that the buildings are very inflammable. The third reason is that because it is on flat land it requires tremendous strength to defend it. For these reasons, my policy or plan was to leave Manila outside the combat zone.

Yamashita's assessment is quite strange considering the fact that he was ignoring many of the advantages that Manila offered to a defender. First, the buildings, as had been mentioned, were not inflammable. Many were earthquake-proof, solid structures. The city, although on flat land, was in military parlance known as a built up area. Thus there were many obstructions to an attacking force. This gave a tremendous advantage to the defender and, therefore, contradicts what Yamashita was stating about using "tremendous strength" to defend Manila. Actually, a hodgepodge force of Japanese sailors, workers, etc., held out for one month against a vastly superior American and Filipino army.

It is obvious in his plan that the objective was that in order to delay the next American attack, it would be necessary to deny him the means to carry it out. Hence, Japanese forces were deployed in such a manner as to interdict or pose a threat to the air base facilities at Clark and the port infrastructure of Manila. Lt. General Akira Muto, the Japanese 14th Area Army Chief of Staff, elaborated that the plan was to establish

> ...three major bases in the mountains east of Manila, the mountains west of Clark Field, and the Baguio-Balete Pass mountain, the Area Army will strike in concert from all directions to check the American forces advancing into central Luzon and the enemy's progress from Luzon to Japan proper or elsewhere.

In line with this, General Yamashita organized the Japanese forces into three main groups. The main body, Shobu had the Japanese 14th Area Army Headquarters, General Yamashita himself, and 152,000 men. Its area of concern was roughly the Northern mountainous region of Luzon. The second group was Kembu which was situated at Clark and Bataan and numbered approximately 30,000 men. It was commanded by Maj. General Rikuchi Tsukada. The Shimbu group controlled Manila and the rest of Southern Luzon numbered 80,000 men and was commanded by General Shizuo Yokoyama.

Sometime during the middle of December, an operational agreement was reached between the Imperial Army and Navy regarding Luzon. The agreement stated that:

> ...the naval force assigned to the defense of Manila was to be placed under the command on Gen. Kobayashi, commander of the Army's Manila Defense Force which was under the Shimbu Group...The Navy's sector for the defense of Manila was the area south of the Pasig River, Nichols Field, the McKinley area and the water front ...Further in accordance with the agreement, the 31st Special Base Force headquarters undertook the construction of defense installations in Manila city in the

latter part of December, and after assigning the zone of action to each battalion, it commenced construction of positions within these zones and planned the establishments of position chiefly to counter enemy attacks from the waterfront and the southwest.

Eventually Gen. Kobayashi withdrew to Montalban with 14 battalions of crack troops, and the Manila Defense command went to Rear Admiral Sanji Iwabuchi, the commander of the 31st Special Base Force. Four sectors were created in Manila. These were the North Sector (more than 4,500 troops) composed of two battalions of Army men north, of the Pasig River. The East Sector (attached to North Sector) composed of one independent naval battalion. The central Sector (more than 5,000 troops and Iwabuchi commanded) composed of the 1st, 2nd, and 5th naval battalions deployed in the districts south of the river. The south sector (more than 5,000 troops) composed of the 3rd and 4th deployed at Nichols Field and Fort McKinley with one army unit under the delegated command of this sector operating at the shore of Laguna de Bay. Expecting a southern advance to the city, the Japanese had erected a heavy defensive belt to meet it, known as the Genko Line. It was composed of pill boxes as emplacements for heavy artillery. The city itself had minefields, pill boxes, bunkers, and tunnels that connected fortified buildings to one another.

Unfortunately for the Japanese, because of the ad-hoc nature of the 16,000 men Manila Defense Force, which was mainly composed of half-trained troops, the defenses were not well coordinated.

JAPANESE UNITS AND DISPOSITION

IMPERIAL GENERAL HQ

SOUTHERN ARMY	SOUTHWEST AREA FLEET
Field Marshal H. Terauchi	VAdm. D. Okochi

14TH AREA ARMY

Gen. Tomoyuki Yamashita

SHOBU ARMY GROUP

Gen. T. Yamashita

SHIMBU ARMY GROUP	KEMBU ARMY GROUP
Gen. Shizuo Yokoyama	Gen. K. Tsukada

MANILA NAVAL DEFENSE FORCE	KOBAYASHI GROUP
RAdm. Sanji Iwabuchi	Gen. Takashi Kobayashi

ASSESSMENT OF THE JAPANESE DEFENSE PLAN

In contrast to the earlier 1941 U.S. defense plan, the Japanese version was pure suicide, plain and simple.

There was no hope so Yamashita was torn between making his army die a glorious death, or keep it alive in the hope that it would tie down U.S. forces.

Unfortunately for Yamashita, although fortunately for the survivors of the decimated 14th Area Army, his decision to fight in the hills and mountains made the destruction of his army immaterial to the Allies. In contrast, places of strategic interest to the Americans in Luzon such as the Central Plain with Clark Air Base, Manila, Manila Bay and its islands and Bataan were immediately liberated and furiously fought for if need be. At best, Yamashita could have hoped to bleed the Americans white, but even that was denied him due to the thousands of Filipino guerrillas who made up a considerable portion of the liberating forces. This then allowed the Americans to rest or rotate their troops who were badly in need of it. It may be said that MacArthur in 1941 infinitely was in a better position than Yamashita was in 1945.

REFERENCES

Barker, Arthur James. *Yamashita*. New York: Ballantine Books, 1973.

Connaughton, Richard, et. al. *The Battle for Manila: The most devastating untold story of World War II*. London: Bloomsbury, 1995.

Long, Gavin. *MacArthur as Military Commander*. London: B.T. Batsford Ltd. and D. Van Nostrand Co., Inc., 1969.

Lt. Gen. Akira Muto, Battle Report of General Muto or Muto Memoirs, G-2 GHQ FEC, Translations of Japanese Documents, Vol. II item 20, Washington DC., 1948.

Luzon 1944–1945, http://www.army.mil/cmh-pg/brochures/luzon/72-28.htm

People of the Philippines vs. Shizuo Yokoyama. Japanese War Crimes Trials. Yamashita Testimony, 3526–3527. Philippine National Archives.

Philippine Area Naval Operations, Part IV, January 1945–August 1945. Japanese Monograph No. 114. Military History Section HQ Army Forces East, 1952.

Reports of General MacArthur, Volume II, Part II, Japanese Operations in the South West Pacific Area. Washington DC: 1966.

Smith, Robert Ross. *United States Army in World War II, The War in the Pacific, Triumph in the Philippines*. Washington, D.C: U.S. Army, 1963.

Steinberg, Rafael. *Return to the Philippines*. Alexandria: Time-Life Books, 1979.

The Fall of the Philippines, http://www.ibibho.org/hyperwar/USA/USA-P-PI/

The First Philippine Campaign, 1941–42, Command, May 1997.

World War Two Armed Forces - Orders of Battle and Organizations. http://orbat.com/site/w w2/drleo/013_usa/_4 l_usarmy/philippines/pa.html

Zaloga, Steven. *Tank Battles of the Pacific War 1941–1945*. Hong Kong: Concord Publications, 1995.

Zaloga, Steven. *U.S. Tank Destroyers in Combat*. Hong Kong: Concord Publications, 1996.

To Collaborate or Not to Collaborate: That is the Question

Dr. Augusto V. de Viana

COLLABORATION AND TREASON DEFINED

Collaboration generally refers to the willful acts by a country's citizens assisting its foreign enemy in a time of conflict. These acts of assistance contribute to the weakening of the country enabling the enemy to achieve its conquest and administration. Collaborators operate against their own country's interests and help contribute to its destruction by weakening its capability to resist the enemy or by later helping in its administration under the enemy's control.

Acts of collaboration take many forms such as rendering personal service for the enemy administration and participating in its leadership, providing him the goods and services he needed and by openly siding with the enemy's armed forces in fighting his own people and their allies.

Collaboration becomes punishable when it becomes treasonable. Treasonable collaboration or just plain treason is defined in Article 114 of the Revised Penal Code of the Philippines. Treason is defined as "an act by any person owing allegiance to the United States[1] or the government of the Philippines, levies war against them or adheres to their enemies, given them aid and comfort within the Philippine Islands or elsewhere."[2]

The revised Penal Code punishes citizens convicted of treason with penalties which range from *reclusion perpetua* or 30 years imprisonment to death and a payment of a fine not exceeding 20,000. Likewise, aliens residing in the Philippines who committed acts of treason can be punished with *prision mayor* or six years and one day to death.

THE CLASSES OF COLLABORATORS DURING WORLD WAR II

During the Second World War many Filipinos collaborated with the Japanese invaders. They could be classified into the following: the political collaborators, the economic collaborators, cultural collaborators, and the military collaborators.

To the first category belonged people who served the Japanese in their political positions. Included among them were officials of the Philippine government under the Japanese occupation such as Jose P. Laurel who served in the Philippine Executive Committee and later became President of the Philippines in 1943. Others were Jorge B. Vargas, the head of the Philippine Executive Commission who later became Philippine ambassador to Japan; Manuel Roxas, Elpidio Quirino, Benigno Aquino, Sr., Camilo Osias, Rafael Alunan, Jr., Claro M. Recto, and others who served in the Philippine Executive Committee and later in the Japanese-sponsored Philippine Republic. Others were the governors, mayors, assemblymen, and councilors. The reasons for their collaborations varied: that they were just following the orders of President Manuel Quezon just before he left for exile; that they were forced to collaborate by the Japanese; that they needed to survive, physically and economically; that they voluntarily or willingly cooperated to pursue their political ambitions and because they sincerely believed in Japan's objectives.

Economic collaborators were those who collaborated to ensure their economic survival. Many of them included scrap metal dealers who sold materials that could be made into armaments and munitions and those who maintained brothels for the Japanese Imperial forces.

They were motivated more by their selfish objectives unlike some collaborators who cooperated out of fear.

Cultural collaborators were those who served the Japanese as their propaganda tools. The Japanese who believed that the country should be exorcised of decadent western culture might have encouraged some of them. These collaborators such as poets Lope K. Santos and Aurelio Alvero cooperated with the Japanese to popularize Filipino culture which was eclipsed by American influences. Other cultural collaborators were also used in the pacification campaign of the Japanese in order to convince the Filipinos to cooperate with Japan.

The last category of collaborators was the military collaborators who consisted of individuals who served with the Japanese forces and helped them in their conquest and control of the country. In these ranks of collaborators were members of groups like the MAKAPILI (Malayang Kalipunan ng mga Pilipino), the Kaigun Hatai, United Nippon or Yoin, Palaaks, and the Borong Borong Gang. Many of these individuals bore arms for the Japanese and served as their guides and informants. Their collaboration resulted in the deaths of fellow Filipinos who were suspected of being anti-Japanese. While many of them may have believed in the sincerity of Japan's aims in the Philippines, many of them were opportunists who saw service with the Japanese as a means of physical and economic survival. Some of them, like the members of the Japanese-sponsored Bureau of Constabulary, were recruited because they needed a source of livelihood.

Since not all Filipinos could resist the Japanese, they evacuated to the mountains. They had to deal in some way or another with the invaders.

BRAVADO AND FEAR

Before the outbreak of the Second World War, there was insufficient preparation for the country's defense. Commonwealth officials however boasted that there would be no compromise with dishonor; that the country would defy any foreign invader. In a speech before the Philippine Military Academy in March 1941, then–Defense Secretary Teofilo Sison said that the Philippines would not negotiate or surrender, but would fight for its freedom. For all his bravado many Commonwealth officials, Sison included, would emerge as one of the leading pro-Japanese collaborators.[3]

Following the first attacks and landings by the Japanese in 1941, Filipino leaders correctly feared that that the combined Filipino and American forces would be defeated and they would have to deal with the Japanese invaders. Aware of his responsibilities in the inevitable dealing with the Japanese, Laurel asked Quezon as to what extent he would deal with the invaders. Vargas also asked the same question and Quezon grasped the significance of Laurel's query and felt that the best man to answer that question was General MacArthur. MacArthur's reply was that nothing could be done about the imminent fall of the Philippines. He said, "Under International Law the occupying army must govern and rule and you cannot do anything but to obey what they tell you to do. Do anything except one thing, that is take the oath of allegiance to the Japanese. If you do (speaking to Vargas), we will shoot you when we come back."

Having received MacArthur's advice, Quezon instructed Laurel and Vargas to do anything in their power to minimize the people's sufferings and cooperate with the Japanese in every way short of taking an oath of allegiance to them. On 24 December, Quezon and his party left for Corregidor leaving practically all the effective control of the Commonwealth government on the shoulders of Vargas.

With information reaching him that Japanese units may enter Manila anytime, Vargas acted swiftly to prevent any untoward incidents between the civilian population and the Japanese Imperial Army. He called Laurel and told him of his plan to have a representative from the central government to meet the Japanese coming from the south of the city. On 30 December, Vargas, Laurel, and General Arsenio Natividad accompanied by the Japanese Consul General Jitaro Kihara and his assistant met the first contingent of Japanese troops at Biñan, Laguna.[4] The three Filipino officials became the first high-ranking Philippine government representatives to meet the Japanese invaders.

On 2 January 1942, the first Japanese units entered Manila proper and the following day, Lt. General Masaharu Homma, the commander-in-chief of the Imperial forces declared the end of American sovereignty in the Philippines and proclaimed martial law in all occupied areas. He announced that the Japanese expeditionary force came to liberate the peoples of Asia from the oppression of colonial powers and enjoined the Filipinos "to sever their relations with the United States, obey faithfully the commands of the Japanese military authorities, to cooperate with them in their activities and to supply them with military needs when asked." Public officials were told to remain at their posts and carry out faithfully their duties as during the Commonwealth administration and all laws during the erstwhile regime would remain in force. The Japanese announcement also revealed a stern warning of severe punishment for hostile acts against the Japanese such as rumor-mongering and disturbance of peace.[5]

On 4 January 1942, Secretary Quintin Paredes received an invitation from General Misami Maeda, Gen. Homma's chief of staff telling him that the Filipino leaders should cooperate with the Japanese in the task of reestablishing peace and order and to stop the widespread looting that had taken place after the city's evacuation by the USAFFE and to prevent hunger among the people. More importantly, Maeda expressed Japan's desire to have a committee formed by Filipinos who were willing and ready to organize a national government with the cooperation of the Japanese Military Administration.[6]

Paredes replied saying that the Filipino leaders were prepared to collaborate with the Japanese in the reestablishment of peace and order and in pleading with the people to return to normal life. However, he demurred on the issue of forming a national government with the cooperation of the Japanese authorities saying that Quezon was still the leader of the Filipino people. Gen. Maeda dismissed Paredes' argument pointing out that the Commonwealth President was out of the question since he was not in Manila.

Paredes later met with Vargas and other Filipino officials at Speaker Jose Yulo's house in Paco, Manila, where they discussed possible actions in dealing with the Japanese. Nine meetings were held there from 5 January to 23 January 1942. All those present in the meetings expressed their loyalty to Quezon. To get the Filipino political elite to cooperate with them, the Japanese authorities under Gen. Maeda conducted separate meetings with Filipino leaders like Vargas, Aquino, Claro M. Recto, and others during which he reiterated his country's wish that the prominent leaders form a committee through which the desires of the Japanese Military Administration could be fulfilled.

When Maeda met with Vargas on 6 January, Vargas was presented with a draft of an appeal to the people to return peacefully to their normal lives and promising them the continuation of public services such as transportation, garbage collection, medical services and the procurement of materials and services for the Japanese army.

The Japanese considered the draft as unsatisfactory. They wanted the unqualified allegiance of the Filipinos. Paredes saw the request for their cooperation as an opportunity to demand independence from the Japanese and to establish a republic that would be recognized by Japan. He also said that the formation of such a republic might be used by Japan to notify the world that the Philippines had abandoned its loyalty to the United States. Bocobo said that collaboration with the Japanese should be limited only to the functions discharged by the Civilian Emergency Agency, an office which was established before the war to take charge in keeping public order among civilians and the delivery of basic services such as sanitation, health, electricity and potable water.[7]

In the afternoon of 7 January, Vargas met with Gen. Maeda who was informed that he was ready to accept Japanese requests in the draft proposal. In return, Maeda said that he would recognize Vargas as the Mayor of Greater Manila. The next day, Vargas, accompanied by Recto, Laurel, Yulo, and Paredes, paid a courtesy call to Gen. Homma and asked for instructions for the administration of Greater Manila. Homma repeated his desire to have a national or central government formed to control and supervise the provinces and municipalities controlled by the Japanese armed forces.

In response to Homma's request, Vargas presented him the proposal of Filipino leaders to form a provisional Commonwealth government which had been discussed the day before. Homma was agreeable to the arrangement. It received a favorable response from the Japanese Military Administration after consulting with the Japanese Ministry of Foreign Affairs. This agreement between Vargas and the Japanese opened the door for collaboration by Filipino leaders.

Though the door had been opened for the collaboration with the Japanese by the country's political elite, on how much cooperation they would provide the Japanese Military Administration, was still to be discussed. They were still hesitant to cooperate with the invaders with MacArthur's threat of punishment still very fresh in their minds, especially if they become too involved with the Japanese by swearing allegiance to them. Vargas and his group had to come up with the form of government that they were to establish. Meanwhile, the Japanese were getting impatient in getting them to cooperate by having them form a national government.

Vargas consulted with Speaker Jose Yulo who was the highest elected official left behind by Quezon. On 8 January, he and the other leaders discussed Homma's desire to have a national government as quickly as possible. They again discussed three proposals on the type of government they might establish: first, a continuation of the Commonwealth government on provisional status as earlier proposed by Yulo; second, a government proposed by Bocobo with the powers of the Civilian Emergency Agency which will be limited to providing administrative and basic services to the people; and the third proposal was the establishment of a Philippine Republic under the guidance of the Japanese Military Administration as proposed by Paredes.

Bocobo objected to the last proposal because such republic established under the aegis of the Japanese would likely be a puppet government similar to those prevailing in occupied China and Manchukuo. Bocobo who was more fearful of the United States said, that "such a republic would alienate the Filipinos from the United States." The group agreed to adopt Yulo's proposal which is the continuation of a Commonwealth government on a provisional status.[8]

When the proposal was presented by the Japanese, Gen. Maeda rejected it because the government proposed by Yulo was a continuation of the Philippine Commonwealth which was a creation of the United States, and Quezon as its President, was himself against the Japanese. With Maeda's rejection the Filipino leaders had to deliberate again on the form of government.

Vargas and other leaders met again to continue discussing on the form of government they would establish under the Japanese. Vargas informed the group that a representative of Gen. Maeda had visited him and that the General wanted to meet the Filipino political leaders with a sworn statement pledging their full cooperation with the Japanese Military Administration. Vargas replied that he was opposed to the word "swear," mindful of MacArthur's warning and that The Hague Convention does not require the inhabitants of an occupied country to swear allegiance or take an oath of loyalty to their military occupants.[9] The Japanese representative said the military authorities were aware of that provision in The Hague Convention and would not compel the Filipinos to take an oath of loyalty. He also suggested that they elect a spokesman in their meetings with the Japanese and that they constitute themselves into a Council of State. Vargas was recognized as the leader of the group and lead negotiator with the Japanese. The response was presented to the Japanese Military Administration on 23 January 1942, formally inaugurating the period of collaboration with the Japanese.

The following day, 24 January, the Council of State had its first meeting at Malacañang Palace to discuss the rules of organization which was drafted by Paredes and Ramon Diokno. During that meeting, Vargas appointed Laurel, Paredes, and Marabut to compose a committee to lay down the rules and regulations concerning the organization of the Council of State which was unanimously approved by the group. The Council selected among themselves the persons who would compose the cabinet of the central administrative organization of the wartime Philippine government which became the Philippine Executive Commission.[10] Benigno Aquino was appointed as Commissioner of the Interior; Jose P. Laurel, Justice; Rafael R. Alunan, Agriculture and Commerce; Quintin Paredes, Public

Works and Communications; Claro M. Recto, Education, Health and Public Welfare; Serafin Marabut, Executive Commissioner; and Teofilo Sison, Auditor General and Chief of the Budget. Not everyone was willing to accept positions in the occupation government. Yulo, who was reluctant to accept an appointment in the Commission, was appointed Chief Justice of the Supreme Court. In this way, according to Vargas, he will be less likely to be pressured by the Japanese.[11]

Vargas later appointed a consultative body that would give advice to the Commission. This was composed of Ramon Avanceña, Alejandro Roces, Miguel Unson, and Emilio Aguinaldo. With the formation of a provisional government and the designation of positions, the Filipino leaders can now collaborate with the Japanese.[12]

The Japanese exploited the formation of a Filipino government under their administration for propaganda purposes. On 28 January 1942, Radio Tokyo broadcast news that a provisional government headed by Filipinos under the Japanese had been formed. Gen. MacArthur voiced his concern to Quezon about such officials joining the enemy administration. Quezon assured MacArthur that the officials who accepted positions in the Japanese-controlled government were merely following his instructions to protect the civilian population and that the group would be limited in performing administrative functions.[13]

BEGINNING OF COLLABORATION

Filipino political collaboration with the Japanese formally began on 26 January 1942 with the establishment of the Philippine Executive Commission. At first, Filipino political leaders were wary of coming out openly to serve in the wartime government, fearful of violating their allegiance to the Commonwealth government and the United States which would cause their punishment as traitors if the Americans returned. However, some members of the Executive Commission and the Council of State such as Jose Yulo and Quintin Paredes believed that the people already marked them as traitors because they were very visible in dealing with the Japanese.

On the other hand, Laurel believed that the United States had failed in protecting the country especially after the fall of Corregidor, and had not prepared the Filipinos to defend themselves from the Japanese invasion. As a consequence, he believed that the sovereignty of the United States over the Philippines had disappeared. It was useless to resist the Japanese and they had to bow to the wishes of the Japanese Military Administration.

As the Japanese occupation wore on, some Filipinos came forward to collaborate with the invaders. They were driven by various motives for their collaboration. Some would collaborate out of patriotism and believed that the country needed their services during its difficult period. Others collaborated because of personal ambition, feeling that the time has come to pursue their political fortunes after being eclipsed by prewar leaders like Manuel Quezon and Sergio Osmeña who had fled the country early in the war. While others were propelled by the desire to get rich quickly by trading with the enemy, some satisfied themselves by serving as spies and informers of the Japanese. There were some who collaborated out of fear for their lives or under pressure from the Japanese. Others, like the guerrillas, resisted and paid with their lives, the collaborators cooperated with the enemy. The underlying reason of their motives was undoubtedly physical survival.

Among the political collaborators Benigno Aquino and Camilo Osias were the most visible. As officials of the Kapisanan sa Paglilingkod sa Bagong Pilipinas (KALIBAPI) which was launched on 30 December 1942, Aquino and Camilo Osias urged the people to discard the practice of shaking hands which they considered as unsanitary. They recommended replacing this gesture with what they called the KALIBAPI salute which was similar to the salute of the Italian fascists and the

German Nazis. Osias who was the Deputy Commissioner of Education in the Executive Commission ordered that the KALIBAPI salute be adopted in all private and public schools and colleges.[14]

Vargas and Aquino berated the people for being fence-sitters during a meeting in Malabon. As Chairman of the KALIBAPI, Vargas expressed confidence that all members are enthusiastic supporters of the New Philippines. Aquino, who was the KALIBAPI Secretary-General, scolded the intellectual and well-to-do elements for their complacency and accused them of being "fence-sitters" in speeches he made in several towns. He also criticized those in government for failing to take "an open and courageous stand, calling them "more American than the Americans themselves in the defense of American sovereignty."[15]

Aquino was more vigorous compared to Vargas in expressing support for Japan. Since his installation as Director-General of the KALIBAPI, he stumped the countryside to gain more adherents to the organization. A large bulk of its membership came from his home province of Tarlac. Aquino acted more vigorously than the other officials and his actions as KALIBAPI chief were propelled by him voluntarily rather than being compelled by the Japanese. For his vigorous cooperation,

Aquino received countless death threats but he said that these meant nothing to him.

Aquino even encouraged the Filipinos to fight for Japan and promised to commit Filipino citizens to fight side by side with the Japanese. Aquino was perceived by his colleagues in the Executive Commission to have gone overboard in expressing his cooperation and enthusiasm for the Japanese. According to Vargas and the others, Aquino was acting on his own. Vargas once complained, "I can't understand why he acts this way. His actions border on servility."[16]

After the war when he was facing treason charges before the People's Court in 1945, Aquino was one of those claiming to have saved the life of Manuel A. Roxas from execution by the Japanese and worked for his release from the concentration camp in Bukidnon on 18 August 1943.

Aside from the political elite who served with Quezon in the Commonwealth years, other political collaborators included the Tagalog poet Benigno Ramos who was Quezon's nemesis. Ramos had founded the Sakdal Party in 1930 which figured in a short but abortive uprising in 1935. Following the uprising, Ramos disowned the actions of the Sakdal and founded another group, the GANAP which was avowedly pro-Japanese. Ramos believed that the Japanese would come to liberate the country from the American imperialists and their Filipino stooges. Ramos went on to found the Malayang Kalipunan ng mga Pilipino or MAKAPILI in December 1944. The MAKAPILI operated independently of the Philippine government headed by President Jose P. Laurel and took orders from the Japanese. Another prominent political collaborator was the lawyer Pio Duran who was a staunch believer of Japan's liberating role. He co-founded the MAKAPILI and served as chief of its military training section.

Another group of collaborators considered as economic collaborators was composed of businessmen and some politicians who found opportunities to amass wealth. They served as suppliers of strategic materials and other items needed by the Japanese for their war effort. Many of them became millionaires overnight as procurers and agents of materials like scrap iron, copper ore, construction materials, labor, conversion of plantations for needed products, and even as recruiters of women "to entertain" and provide relief for war-weary Japanese soldiers.[17] Some of the notorious collaborators were Vice President Sergio Osmeña's son, Sergio Jr., and Francisco de la Rama who sold scrap metals and machine parts to the Japanese. Aside from amassing wealth, the Japanese rewarded economic collaborators by giving them privileges such as the ownership of automobiles which had to be requested from the Japanese authorities as all motor vehicles were commandeered by the military.[18]

Cultural collaborators served as staff of magazines and newspapers which the Japanese utilized as outlets for their propaganda. Among these people were prominent writers like Camilo Osias and Lope K. Santos. One of them was the prominent radio personality Dely (Tia Dely) Magpayo who worked with the Hodobu, the Japanese propaganda arm. The encouragement of Filipino culture by the Japanese led to its blossoming. Culture was a means of attracting popular support.

Other collaborators who can be considered as non-political were the members of the police force and those of the Japanese-led Bureau of Constabulary (BOC) which were composed of former USAFFE officers and men. Some of these men were pressed into the service of the Japanese while others joined voluntarily because they needed a source of livelihood.[19] There was also the association known as the KALIBAPI (Kapisanan sa Paglilingkod sa Bagong Pilipinas) which was established on 30 December 1942 to replace all political parties and civic organizations. The KALIBAPI had around 350,000 members in 1943. Among its members were government employees who were told that they would lose their jobs if they did not join it. The KALIBAPI had two youth arms, the *Kabataang Maghahanda* for the young people aged seven to 15 years old and the *Kabataang Katulong* for those who were aged 16 to 18. The KALIBAPI was formed ostensibly to work for national unity since the interests of the community are above self-consideration, and to develop among the people virtues such as patriotism, self-reliance, bravery, discipline, self-sacrifice and hard work. Although on the surface, these were worthwhile objectives, they were intended to develop a docile population that suited the agenda of the occupying power in the Philippines. In addition the KALIBAPI was intended by the Japanese to enjoin the opposition, particularly the guerrillas, to embrace the merits of its new order called the Greater East Asia Co-Prosperity Sphere.[20]

Aside from the KALIBAPI, there were also the District and Neighborhood Associations or DANAS which were established in the barrios in August 1942 to maintain peace and order. These were spy organizations because their duties were to report to the authorities the presence of suspicious persons and to help the Constabulary in their arrest. The DANAS also prepared a census of all inhabitants within their area and conducted periodic surveys to check their movements.

As for the military collaborators, there were Filipinos who formed units to support the Japanese. These were the Ganaps, the Palaaks, United Nippon, the Pampars and the Makapilis. The GANAPs were led by Benigno Ramos, a Tagalog writer, and demagogue who styled himself as the *Tandis* or Supreme Leader of the Sakdal movement in the 1930s. His followers launched a brief but bloody uprising against the government on 2–3 May 1935. Though officially abolished by the Japanese, the Ganap organization continued to exist and its members served as informers of the Japanese.

The Palaaks were also known as the Bamboo Army because they were armed with bamboo spears. They were organized by the Japanese army even before the inauguration of the Philippine Republic in 1943 and were recruited from the various neighborhood associations in the different towns. Like the Ganaps, they served as spies and informers of the Japanese. The United Nippon, also known as the *Yoin*, was a military organization and an adjunct of the Ganap. They were trained by Japanese officers and wore Japanese army uniforms and were equipped with Japanese rifles. The Pampars which stood for *Pambansang Pag-asa ng mga Anak ni Rizal*, were civilian collaborators organized by Crisostomo Pendon, a resident of Pililia, Rizal. Like the United Nippon, the Pampars were trained in combat tactics and armed by the Japanese. They wore denim uniforms and short pants and served as sentries of Japanese camps. They served as combat troops whenever necessary.[21]

Already mentioned was the MAKAPILI which was established mainly by General Artemio Ricarte, Benigno Ramos and Pio Duran. The Makapilis were the most potent of the military collaborators. Its members received salaries from the Japanese and numbered in the thousands. The Makapili organization was launched in Manila on 8 December 1944. Its leaders were Ricarte, Ramos, Duran, youth leader Aurelio Alvero, Leon Villafuerte and Andres Villanueva. Aside from acting as a spy network for the Japanese, the Makapilis actively participated in the suppression of the resistance movement including the arrest, torture and mass executions of guerrilla suspects. There were similar Makapili-type organizations which were either its subgroups or entirely independent organizations such as the Borong-Borong gang, Kaigun Hatai and the Nishimura Butai were responsible for terrorizing the civilian population and the deaths of suspected guerrillas during the Japanese occupation.[22]

Adding to these armed pro-Japanese collaborators were criminal elements, individual spies, informers, and servants of the Japanese whom the Japanese recruited to fight on their side.

Many of these pro-Japanese Filipinos genuinely believed that Japan came to liberate the Philippines from western imperialism and in Japan's aims of co-prosperity. They joyfully welcomed the Japanese units as they entered "Japan towns" like Cabuyao, Biñan, and Santa Rosa in Laguna. They were gladdened that the Japanese had brown skins like Filipinos and were therefore treated as racial brothers. During the war, these collaborators served as guides and informers of the Japanese. In some instances, they figured in battles against the guerrillas and the American forces. During the battle for Manila in February 1945, they were given orders to defend the city to the last and were seen helping the Japanese burn and pillage the city. With the American onslaught many military collaborators especially the MAKAPILIS, melted into the population and were sought after by the guerrillas.

Collaborators lived a life of relative ease during the Japanese occupation. While most of the civilian population was suffering from hunger and malnutrition, they profited from their association with the enemy. It was said that just after the war, it was easy to distinguish a collaborator from a non-collaborator. Right after World War II one Congressman remarked:[23]

> ...During the Japanese occupation, I should like to say that the collaborator was easy to distinguish and to know. If you see a husky fellow and most of them—not all may be (sic) who has the pep in life,

*fat with big and bulging pockets, you can be sure
that he is a collaborator.*

The Japanese again tried to require all government
officials to swear allegiance to Japan with the issuance
of Military Order No. 5. According to them this was
needed to erase the reliance on Europe and America and
in particular, the idolization of the United States which
should be eradicated with the friendship with Japan
based upon the awakening of Filipinos as Orientals.[24]
The Executive Commission considered this move as a
violation of The Hague Convention which prohibits the
forcing of the inhabitants of an occupied territory to
swear allegiance to their occupying powers. An impasse
ensued as the Japanese insisted that all government
officials and employees take an oath of loyalty. A
compromise was reached after the Executive Commission
agreed that the government officials swear[25] loyalty to
the Japanese Imperial forces but not to Japan itself.[26]

THE JAPANESE LURE OF PHILIPPINE INDEPENDENCE

The most important enticement of the Japanese to
solicit the support of Filipino leaders was their promise
of independence for the Philippines. Japan promised
to grant the Philippines its independence when it
deemed that the country supported its objectives. These
"independent" countries were puppet governments that

would become Japan's allies against its enemies. Only the gullible or extremely pro-Japanese believed that the Philippines could become truly free—courtesy of Japan.

Most of the Filipino officials in the Executive Commission knew Japan's plans and were just playing along. They believed that the Philippines can never be free under the sponsorship of the Japanese but at least it could be nominally free to resist Japan's efforts to involve the Filipinos in its war against the Allies. On 29 January 1943, the Commission met and voted to send a message thanking Tojo for his promise of independence for the Philippines in the soonest possible time.

On 8 February, Vargas had a crowd of 300,000 conduct a gratitude rally for Japan's promise of independence. The rally was very significant because the attendance of a large number of people and the appearance of prominent Filipino leaders expressing their cooperation and support for the Japanese Military Administration. It sent a message to the people that it was alright to cooperate with the enemy. Soon officials both high and low competed with each other in expressing their gratitude to Japan. Thus Filipino allegiance to the United States and the Philippine Commonwealth was temporarily set aside.

On the surface the Filipinos would show their adherence to Japan's objectives by attending the KALIBAPI rallies and participating in its activities. Behind the backs of the Japanese Filipinos showed their opposition through the best way they knew—humor. They called the KALIBAPI by another name: KALIBABI—"babi" being the Pampango word for "pig." Sometimes they called the organization Kapisanan ng Paglikom ng mga Baboy ("organization to collect pigs.") Often they might remark to each other if one belongs to the KALIBAPI, the answer would be *"No, sa kabila pa"*—meaning that he still belongs to the "other side"—meaning the Americans. The official government radio station PIAM was nicknamed Putang Ina ang Maniwala ("one who believes this radio station is a son of bitch"). On the Japanese greetings of "Banzai!" they would cry out "Bangkay"—Tagalog for "corpse."

Benigno Ramos knew that the Filipinos were not sincere in collaborating with Japan. Ramos reportedly told the Japanese that the Filipinos were not sincere in cooperating with them and that they were 95% pro-American and 5% liars. He also told the people during a rally that he would have Laurel hanged if he had his way.[27]

THE ROAD TO INDEPENDENCE

On 19 June 1943 the Preparatory Committee for Philippine Independence was formed. It was composed of Emilio Aguinaldo, Antonio de las Alas, Rafael Alunan, Jr., Jose P. Laurel, Benigno Aquino Sr., Melecio Arranz, Ramon Avanceña, Manuel C. Briones, Vicente Madrigal, Camilo Osias, Quintin Paredes, Claro M. Recto, Manuel Roxas, Pedro Sabido, Sultan sa Ramain, Teofilo Sison, Emiliano Tria Tirona, Miguel Unson, Jorge B. Vargas, and Jose Yulo. The committee was enlarged to include Serafin Marabut, Elpidio Quirino, Esteban de la Rama, Guillermo Francisco, Pio Duran, Eulogio Rodriguez, Sr., Artemio Ricarte, Leon Guinto, Archbishop Gabriel Reyes, and Bishop Enrique Sobrepeña.

On the following day, the PCPI was formally launched with the induction of its members by Gen. Shigeru Kuroda, the Commander-in-Chief of the Japanese Military Administration. The PCPI drafted a new Constitution as the Commonwealth Constitution was discarded because it was a creation of the Americans. The drafting committee was formed with Jorge B. Vargas as Chairman. Its members consisted of Rafael Alunan, Camilo Osias, Emilio Aguinaldo, and Vicente Madrigal. Jose P. Laurel, the President of the PCPI, could not attend the initial proceedings because he was recovering from serious wounds from an assassination attempt by guerrillas while playing golf at Wack-Wack in Mandaluyong.

The Constitution was finished at the end of August and signed by the members of the PCPI during a ceremony on 6 September 1943. Two days later, it was "ratified" by a general assembly consisting of 117 KALIBAPI members. During the plenary session of the National Assembly on 20 September, Laurel was elected President of the new Republic while Aquino was elected Speaker. On 14 October 1943, the Philippine Republic was inaugurated. The inauguration was attended by "500,000 to 800,000 people" according to the *Tribune*. On the same day, notices were sent to 27 countries requesting them to recognize the new Philippine Republic. It was recognized by both Axis, Axis-occupied and neutral countries like Germany, Italy, Burma, Siam, Manchukuo, the Japanese-sponsored Chinese Republic under Wang Ching Wei, as well as Spain, Portugal, Slovenia, Serbia, and Croatia. Predictably, Japan was the first to recognize the Philippine Republic. In the evening, Laurel asked the United States to recognize the new Republic.

The Filipinos expected that Japan might demand a pact of alliance that would require Filipinos to fight the Allies. Claro M. Recto who had become the Republic's Foreign Minister submitted a Pact of Alliance which afforded all kinds of facilities for Japan short of committing troops for its defense. Laurel avoided the Japanese demand for a declaration of war against the United States and instead declared an amnesty for the guerrillas.

Laurel's actions were the beginning of their disillusionment with him. Nevertheless, they avoided any confrontation with him because they felt that he might still be useful in the future. Laurel, on the other hand, used whatever power in his hands to spare the people from greater suffering and moderate the Japanese demands. After assuming the Presidency of the country, he immediately expelled his "adviser" Consul General Kihara. Laurel later proved to be more difficult to handle than his predecessor, Vargas.

Laurel knew that the 1943 republic is not a free one. He did not know, however, consider such republic as a sham. It was one complete with sovereign powers though the Japanese exercised a pervasive influence over it. Laurel bravely used the powers in the presidency to prevent a worse situation and refused to be cowed down by the Japanese. When the Japanese finally demanded a declaration of war following the first American air attacks in September 1944, he instead issued Proclamation No. 30 declaring the existence of a state of war between the Philippines and the United States. This proclamation was a useless document being remained unratified by the National Assembly who had been dismissed. A true statesman, Laurel owned this responsibility as his alone and insulated the others from possible retribution by the Americans.

THE ARREST AND TRIAL OF THE COLLABORATORS

With the return and subsequent victory of the Americans over the Japanese, Filipino collaborators were rounded up and detained. Among them were political, economic and military collaborators. With the exception of Laurel and Vargas who were detained in Sugamo Prison in Japan, most of the political collaborators were imprisoned at Iwahig.

American treatment of the collaborators was unequal. Collaborators like Manuel Roxas were "liberated" while others like Recto, Yulo, and Aquino were arrested and jailed. MacArthur, who was Roxas' friend, said that Roxas was an American military agent. Others like Yulo and Alunan also claimed the same role but were ignored. By arbitrarily exonerating Roxas and reinstating him in the U.S. Army, MacArthur legitimized his friend's role in the wartime government and bolstered his credentials in preparation for his return to active politics. Other collaborators had to go through the process of investigation by the U.S. military authorities.

President Sergio Osmeña, who had succeeded Quezon following the latter's death, faced a dilemma following the arrest of the collaborators. Two of his sons, Sergio Jr. and Nicasio were accused as economic collaborators. Osmeña ordered the arrest of his sons and imprisoned them at Iwahig. When Congress reconvened, Senator Mariano J. Cuenco asked for his resignation in connection with the collaboration charges against his sons.[28]

Though the Philippine and American officials were given orders to deal with the collaboration question and prosecute the collaborationists, there were no clear guidelines on how to deal with the problem. Moreover, the Commonwealth government was saddled with more gargantuan problems to deal with the problem of collaborators. A memorandum by Francisco A. Delgado issued on 3 April 1945 defined who were the collaborators. They were the following:

1. Leaders of the puppet government who were responsible for either directly or indirectly for the policy of collaboration with the Japanese;

2. Those who served in said government from bureau directors up, in spite of the knowledge of the government's policy of active collaboration and especially after said

government declared war against the United States;

3. Those who by word, pen, or deed aided the propaganda to further the war aims of the Japanese;

4. Those, not being impelled by strict necessity (i.e. imminent starvation) sold goods or materials to the Japanese; those although impelled in the beginning by strict necessity, later on sold much more than said necessity demanded;

5. Organizers and members of pro-Japanese organizations like the GANAP, KALIBAPI, and the MAKAPILI.

Delgado said that persons liable for prosecution for treason were the following:[29]

1. Government officials—The Executive Commission and the Republic, especially the men at the helm who tried to deceive the people into docile submission to the Japanese, persecuting the guerrillas, sanctioning pro-Japanese groups like the KALIBAPI and the MAKAPILI which were established for

aiding the Japanese army; facilitating the procurement of food and war materials for the Japanese; aided Japanese invaders and made their stay more comfortable; relieving Japanese of governing the country thereby releasing their manpower to its mission of conquest and prosecution of the military occupation;

2. Buy and sell tycoons—Those who were vociferous in their protestation of loyalty to the United States but sold scrap metal and other war materials to allow the Japanese to fight the United States; men whose loyalty withers under the luster of gold and whose strength of conviction cannot stand up to the weight of worthless Japanese war notes;

3. Instruments of pro-Japanese propaganda— Announcers, writers, commentators, producers, directors in pro-Japanese plays who indulged in pro-Japanese campaigns and speeches;

4. Organizers of pro-Japanese societies and associations—GANAP, KALIBAPI, MAKAPILI. Some of them were avowedly pro-Japanese but some were spineless opportunists who

through them saw their chance to fill their pockets and try to satisfy their interest for public recognition by licking the books of the almighty invader;

5. Those in the employ of the Japanese forces—Buyers, purchasing agents who enjoyed cuts and bribes of the buy-and-sell tycoons;

6. Composers and writers of pro-Japanese hymns and songs—Organizers of literary contests who love to be in the limelight, never mind if it scorches them;

7. Scores of supine, egotistic, and unprincipled men who will be exposed as cases come up.

The same memorandum urged the government to take positive action against the "big fishes" to serve as an abject lesson on the importance of loyalty but should not cover the "small fries" with a proclamation of general amnesty.

To prosecute the collaborators, a law was passed creating a People's Court and the Office of Special Prosecutors. The law, Commonwealth Act No. 682 which was crafted by the reconstituted Congress, was called by Lorenzo Tañada, who was appointed as head of the Office of

Special Prosecutors, as "weak and rotten." The law was crafted by former collaborators who resumed their seats in Congress and it allowed only six months from the passage of the law to file cases. The staff of the Court and office of the prosecutors were poorly provided for. Furthermore Tañada found to his dismay that Gen. MacArthur ordered American forces not to become involved in the prosecution of collaborators. Tañada also learned that the financial, legal, and logistical supports he expected from the Americans were not forthcoming because these were diverted to Tokyo for the prosecution of the Japanese war criminals.

Despite these obstacles, the Office of the Special Prosecutors performed its duties well. By the end of the filing period on 19 March 1946, the Office had filed treason cases against 5,556 persons. Among the persons charged were President Jose P. Laurel who had 130 counts of treason and Jorge B. Vargas who had 115 specifications. Other prominent indictees included Benigno Aquino Sr. who had 111 counts of treason; Leon Guinto with 68; Claro M. Recto, 26; Quintin Paredes, 20; Antonio de las Alas, 20, Camilo Osias, 14; Emiliano Tria Tirona, 13; Hilario Moncado, 15; Emilio Aguinaldo, 15; Vicente Madrigal 17; Pedro Sabido, 8; Gen. Guillermo Francisco, 22; Francisco Lozada, 10; and Antonio Torres, 4.[30]

The more than 5,000 cases were divided into batches of 160 at a time and apportioned among the first four divisions. In the Office of Special Prosecutors which had 24 prosecutors, each prosecutor had an average of 232 cases. These cases could take decades to prosecute.

The accused political collaborators provided several arguments for their defense. These were: duress and the preconceived plan of the Japanese; the invalidity of some official acts of the occupation government; the Instructions of President Quezon; the unpreparedness of the United States for the defense of the Philippines; the suspended allegiance of the Filipinos; the very nature of military occupation of a territory; the theories of the abrogation of the political laws of the Philippines and suspended sovereignty. Of these arguments, the defenses of suspended sovereignty, abrogation of political laws and suspended allegiance were thrown out by the Supreme Court.

On the claim of duress the prosecutors said the pressure of coercion must be real and that the collaborators were actually accomplices of the Japanese. Teofilo Sison who used this argument in his trial was found guilty of treason and sentenced to life imprisonment. However he appealed the court's decision to the Supreme Court and was freed on bail.

Of all the cases lodged against the members of the Laurel Cabinet, only that of Teofilo Sison ended in conviction. The cases of Rafael Alunan, Emiliano Tirona, and Gen. Guillermo Francisco were dismissed because of two reasons: the failure of the prosecution to prove their guilt through the two-witness rule and the contention that these officials were just fulfilling their lawful duties. The cases of Jose P. Laurel, Jorge B. Vargas, Claro M. Recto, and Antonio de las Alas eventually ended in dismissals because of the issuance of a presidential amnesty for all political and economic collaborators.

Meanwhile, public sentiment began to shift in favor of the collaborators. In the 1946 elections, many of the winners including that of the Presidency of the Philippines were all collaborators. It drove the message that not all collaborators were traitors. In the People's Court, the justices were increasingly divided as some of them started to manifest collaborationist views. One judge, Antonio Quirino resigned from the Court to become a lawyer for Laurel. Another, Pompeyo Dizon who wrote the decision convicting Teofilo Sison, resigned to resume private practice. There was also some political pressure exerted by President Roxas who during the oath-taking ceremonies of replacement judges said that the duress or coercion by the Japanese is not to be presumed or taken place as a matter of fact by the tribunal but should be proven by the defense. "Treason," he said, "must be viewed as a crime punishable by the country, municipal laws rather than the point of international law." Roxas then cited the example of a guerrilla killed by a civilian of a country under enemy occupation. He said that while under international law, the guerrilla's assailant could not be prosecuted because guerrillas are bandits from the enemy's point of view, yet the person could be tried for a crime under municipal laws when the war is over.[31]

In the Office of Special Prosecutors, the prosecutors had difficulty finding witnesses especially when a powerful person was involved. Many witnesses were bribed or threatened with death as some suddenly developed amnesia or turned hostile to the prosecution. There was also the influence of Filipino culture of "letting bygones be bygones," "to forgive is divine," and "time heals old wounds." There was also a growing anti-American feeling which also influenced the people to ask "why continue prosecuting the collaborators? They committed treason against the United States, not to the Philippines. America, not the Philippines was at war with Japan. It was alright to go after the collaborators when we were still under America. But we are now an independent nation. Let us throw the collaboration cases overboard and forget it once and for all."[32]

There was a belief or rumor that the top officials of the Roxas government were secretly aiding the top collaborators on trial and were pooling funds for their defense.[33]

Despite the many hardships, the People's Court was able to dispose of 1,104 of the 5,556 cases by 4 February 1948. Out of this number only 156 or a mere 0.27% of the total cases ended in convictions. Only the case of Teofilo Sison was politically prominent.

The treason trials developed legal precedents in Philippine jurisprudence. In People Vs. Jose Luis Godinez, the High Tribunal ruled that "...mere governmental work under the enemy is not *per se* treasonable."[34] With the Godinez doctrine, many employees of the government who served the Japanese during the war were benefited. The political collaborators also used the same doctrine in the argument of their cases.

In People Vs. Escleto (47 *Official Gazette* 107), the two-witness rule was upheld by the Supreme Court, rejecting the contention of the People's Court that the separate testimonies were admissible as evidence.[35] The Supreme Court said that the Philippine treason law is based on the American constitution and was made to be severely restrictive so that obtaining convictions for treason would be difficult.

In People Vs. Jose de Castro (L-547), the Supreme Court ruled that the membership in the Bureau of Constabulary during the occupation period was not treasonous.[36]

In People Vs. Perez (L-547), the Supreme Court ruled that "the procurement of women to satisfy the lust of Japanese officers or men or to enliven the entertainment in their honor is not treason even though the women and the entertainment made life more pleasant for the enemies and boost their spirits."[37]

In People Vs. Agoncillo (45 *Official Gazette* 2874), the Supreme Court declared that the sale of material not exclusively for war purposes was not treason and the said sale does not necessarily carry an intention of the vendor to adhere to the enemy.[38]

In another decision, that of People Vs. Abad (44 *Official Gazette* 4901), the Supreme Court ruled that membership in the MAKAPILI and similar organizations was a continuous, indivisible and overt act which gives aid and comfort to the enemy.[39]

THE AMNESTY FOR COLLABORATORS

On 28 January 1948 President Roxas issued Proclamation No. 31 declaring an amnesty for political and economic collaborators. The amnesty proclamation excluded certain classes of collaborators which were: those who took up arms against the allied nations or members of the resistance movement; those who acted voluntarily as spies or informers of the Japanese; and those who committed murder, arson, coercion, physical injuries or any other crime against person or property.

Roxas averred that around 20 to 30% of the treason indictees would be benefit by Proclamation No. 31. He also said that the People's Court would soon be abolished and the treason cases not covered by the proclamation would be transferred to the regular courts of the first instance.

For those who favored it, Proclamation No. 31 would restore unity and minimize the suffering of the people. To those against it, the amnesty was a betrayal for those who fought and suffered during the Japanese occupation. Senator Ramon Diokno, another member in the minority in the Senate, opposed amnesty because of its possibility of what the country would do in the event of another foreign invasion. He said that in the future if the amnesty were approved, there would be no such resistance movements that made the Filipinos famous during the last war. Tañada who had quit as the head of the Office of Special Prosecutors to run as Senator delivered the most stinging criticism of the amnesty. The amnesty confirms the growing belief that this government (Roxas' administration) "is one for big shots and of big shots."[40]

Tañada's remarks were caused by the scope of the amnesty proclamation which limited itself to the political and economic collaborators. The amnesty, if approved, would benefit only about 30% of the indicted collaborators, all of whom consisted of the political elite who served under the Japanese-sponsored government, the economic tycoons who traded with the enemy, the intellectuals who helped in spreading propaganda, entrepreneurs and others who benefited from dealing with the Japanese. The amnesty left out the poor, uneducated and gullible Filipinos who served in the Japanese armed forces and those who served as minor functionaries, informers and spies. Tahada continued his tirade with an analogy: "When a plane carrying big shots crashes, the machinery of the government is mobilized in the rescue of the victims, but if a plane carrying unimportant persons crashes, the same is not done here."[41]

In the House of Representatives questioning by congressmen revealed that the People's Court had disposed of 1,104 cases as of 31 January 1948 out of the 5,553 filed. This left 4,449 cases to be tried. Of the 1,104 cases, none of these had a final judgement except in those where the accused pleaded guilty to the charges.

It would take eight to ten years for the People's Court to clear its dockets. During further questioning on the floor the breakdown of cases before the People's Court according to the type of collaboration as of 4 February 1948 was revealed as follows:[42]

1. Military, BOC, MAKAPILI, Peace Organizations and policemen   2,925

2. Espionage agents, spies and informers   2,677

3. Economic collaborators   355

4. Political collaborators   472

5. Cultural collaborators   100

These figures showed that the scope of the proposed amnesty which covered only the political and economic collaborators was very limited.[43] The issue was raised by the congressmen who said that since Proclamation No. 51 favored only a minority of the collaborators, the proclamation should be declared unconstitutional. Debates on the proclamation dragged on until 13 February as the pro and anti-amnesty lawmakers clashed. Just before the voting on the ratification of the amnesty, Congressman Hermenegildo Atienza eloquently voiced his concern on the effect of the proposed amnesty on the future generations of Filipinos who might be confronted with another foreign invasion. He said:[44]

> *I am worried of the generations still unborn. One day our shores will be trampled upon again by the enemy; one day our skies will darken with the wings of the invaders and we shall wonder, we ask as Rizal once said,' Where is the youth that shall dedicate his golden hour for the defense of the country?' That youth will not be there. The youth will not be there because today, Friday the 13th, we voted forever to establish the utter futility of sacrificing one's blood, sweat and tears for his native land; today we have given a premium on the refusal to fight and willingness to embrace the enemy. Today, we have laid down one abject lesson—To live and to collaborate is to be idealized and glorified.*

After his eloquent speech, 67 congressmen gave concurrence to Proclamation No. 51 with only five against.[45]

THE AFTERMATH AND IMPLICATIONS OF THE COLLABORATION ISSUE

The amnesty resulted in the dismissal of 827 cases of political and economic collaborators. On 14 February

1948, Laurel's case along with that of Vargas, was dismissed.[46] The case of Teofilo Sison which was awaiting appeal before the Supreme Court was dismissed on 26 February 1948.[47] Other indictees like Recto and de las Alas refused to avail of the amnesty and insisted that they be acquitted. This was contrary to the provisions of the amnesty proclamation which said that the indictees could not refuse its benefits. Nevertheless their cases were dismissed by the People's Court after they secured their respective acquittals. Those who were not covered by the amnesty such as the accused military collaborators, including those that committed crimes such as murder, were tried and imprisoned. These collaborators were not from the elite and were mostly the poor and uneducated.

The collaboration issue was not erased with the proclamation of an amnesty. It was subsequently resurrected to be used as an election issue. This took place during the 1949 presidential election when Laurel ran for the presidency of the Philippines against Elpidio Quirino.

The collaboration issue which resurfaced in the election campaign only served to muddle the more important issues such as the lack of good government, extravagance by high officials, the indifference towards the plight of the people, grinding poverty and inequitable distribution of wealth and subservience of the Philippine government to the United States. It only opened old wounds and brought back ugly memories of war years.

During the 1969 presidential campaign, the issue of collaboration during the Second World War was again resurrected. This time it was against Sergio Osmeña, Jr. who was the candidate of the Liberal Party running against incumbent President Ferdinand E. Marcos who was supported by the Nacionalista Party. Osmeña was depicted as a merchant of death and a convicted traitor by Marcos' propaganda machinery.

Former collaborators bore the stigma of being called *kulaboreytors*—a term which carried a characteristic of being a traitor to the country. Parents dissuaded their children from marrying or even associating with *kulaboreytors*, especially former MAKAPILIs. Their descendants were also not spared by the stigma. They were publicly insulted as *anak ng kulaboreytor* or children of Makapilis and buy and sell merchants who served the Japanese. One such story involved a young student named Benigno Aquino, Jr. who was ridiculed by his teacher who called him a son of a collaborator. Aquino, Jr. was the son of Benigno Aquino, Sr., who served as Secretary General of the KALIBAPI.

The stigma of collaboration and the humiliation of imprisonment hardened the bitterness of some politicians especially Claro M. Recto who became one of the strongest critics of Philippine government administrations from Magsaysay to Garcia. Recto believed that the collaboration issue was the fault of the United States, which failed to protect the Philippines yet, demanded undying allegiance from the Filipinos. Recto was later elected senator and criticized the subservience of the Republic to the United States. In his time he advocated the abrogation of unequal treaties with the United States and the institution of nationalist policies that would remove the Philippines from the shadow of America.

Social stigma was the least punishment that could be inflicted on former collaborators especially the military collaborators. Relatives of persons who were killed or tortured by the MAKAPILI and other pro-Japanese groups were reported to have committed acts of revenge against former members. These included ambushes, abductions, and mutilations. Former guerrillas were said to have formed "trigger squads" to hunt down former informers, spies, and other allies of the Japanese even long after the war. Relatives of members of these pro-Japanese groups were reported to have taken means to strike back.

The treatment of the collaboration issue would reflect on the Filipino patriotic values. It showed that collaboration could be rewarded. The disposition of the issue reveals how the nation treats its problems. It does not solve the problems but rather dissolves them, hoping that these would be forgotten. Oftentimes these problems like high-profile ones were not given final closure. These would be resurrected at a convenient time. It reveals a culture of indecision which permeates our history which is unfortunately never learned.

NOTES

[1] With the recognition of Philippine independence by the United States on 4 July 1946, offenses against the United States were removed from the definition of treason.

[2] Luis B. Reyes. *Revised Penal Code Annotated*, Vol. 2., (Manila Rex Book Store, 1985), 1–2.

[3] "No Compromise," *Philippines Free Press*, 22 March 1941.

[4] Ibid., 201.

[5] *Tribune*, 4 January 1942.

[6] Agoncillo, *op. cit.*, 202.

[7] Mauro Garcia, ed., *Documents of the Japanese Occupation of the Philippines*, (Manila: Philippine Historical Association, 1965), 4–7.

[8]   Saulo, *op. cit.*,112–114.

[9]   Garcia, *op. cit.*, 12.

[10] Agoncillo, *The Fateful Years, op. cit.*, 326.

[11] Garcia, *op. cit.*, 37–39.

[12] Ibid., 121–122.

[13] Manuel Luis Quezon, *The Good Fight* (New York: Appleton-Century, 1946), 157–160.

[14] Agoncillo, *Fateful Years, op. cit.*, 499.

[15] Ibid.; National Historical Institute, *Filipinos in History* (Manila: National Historical Institute, 1995), 19–21.

[16] Ibid.

[17] Constantino, *op. cit.*, 125.

[18] "U.S. Treasury Prepares Blacklist of Collaborators; Listed Persons and Business Firms Face Business Curbs," *New York Times*, 8 August 1945.

[19] The Japanese organized the BOC in 1942 by initially recruiting 5,000 men and 100 USAFFE who were just released from detention. The latter served as its officers. Around 1944 the BOC had a force of around 15,000. There were no exact figures about the total force because of the destruction of records at the end of the Second World War.

[20] Ibid., 75.

[21] Carlos Quirino, *The Laurel Story* (Manila: Jose P. Laurel Memorial Corporation, 1992), 103–104.

22 "Treason Mass Trial Proposed," *Manila Times*, 8 August 1946, 1:5.

23 Congressional Record, House of Representatives (Manila: June 1945), 14–18.

24 *Tribune*, 26 February 1943, 3.

25 Laurel Collaboration Papers, S. 4 Box No. 11, Japanese Military Administration Order No. 5, 11 April 1942.

26 Ibid.; See also: Saulo, 197.

27 Abaya, *op. cit.*, p. 236; See also Gregorio F. Zaide, *Documentary Sources of Philippine History*, Vol. 11 (Manila: National Book Store, 1992), 94.

28 "Sen. Cuenco Demands Pres. Osmeña Resignation in Connection with Collaboration Charges Against Sons: Charges 1 Son Paid Father's Debts with Collaboration Profits," *New York Times*, 16 September 1945, 3:5.

29 Ibid., 24–25.

30 "Laurel, Other Top Officials are Indicted, Court to Ask SCAB to Return, Vargas, Others to Islands," *Manila Times*, 1:1.

    Other persons indicted with Laurel were persons in economic collaboration during the war. These were socialite Carmen Planas, Haydee Heras Teehankee, Jose Figueras, Jose Desidero, Jose Robles Jr., Gregorio San Agustin, Jose Y. Ferrer, former Cavite Governor Kamil Hemady, former Representative Jose Veloso, Tomas Opus, Ramon Erenet, Vicente Ybierras, and Ma. Luisa Dominguez, the granddaughter of Gen. Artemio Ricarte.

[31] Ibid.

[32] Leon O. Ty, "I will not Quit," *Philippines Free Press*, 19 October 1946, 6.

[33] Ibid.

[34] *Official Gazette*, Republic of the Philippines, Vol. 45, 2524. Also: People Vs. Jose Luis Godinez (L895). Transcript of decision of the Supreme Court. 31 December 1947, 7 pages, Transcript found among the Laurel War Papers, Laurel Memorial Library.

See also: Luis B. Reyes, *Revised Penal Code*, Book II, 9.

[35] *Official Gazette*, Republic of the Philippines, Vol. 47, 107.

[33] *Official Gazette*, Republic of the Philippines, People Vs. de Castro, Vol. 47, 105.

[37] *Official Gazette*, Republic of the Philippines, People Vs. Perez, Vol. 46, 4886.

[38] *Official Gazette*, Republic of the Philippines, Vol. 45, No. 7, 2874.

[39] *Official Gazette*, Republic of the Philippines, Vol. 44, 4901.

[40] Ibid.

[41] Ibid.

[43] Ibid.

[43] Perez's figures were not accurate. Summed up the total number of cases reached 6,529 instead of the official figure of 5,553. It included the unsubstantiated cases

which were dropped. The exact breakdown of 5,553 cases remained unavailable.

[44] Ibid.

[45] The congressmen who voted against the amnesty proclamation were Damaso Samonte, Mariano Logarta, Carlos Hilado, Adriano Lomuntad, and Ricardo Navarro.

[46] "Laurel Case Dismissed Today," *Manila Chronicle*, 14 February 1948, 1:5.

See also: "Vargas is Freed by P.C." *Manila Chronicle*, 15 February 1948, 1:1.

[47] "Lim Seeks Quashing of Treason Complaints Against 10 Indictees," *Manila Times*, 29 February 1948, 1:7.

Cultural Policies of the Japanese Military Administration

Dr. Luis C. Dery

INTRODUCTION

Japan has been interested in having the Philippines under its rule. Hideyoshi (1537–1598) planned to conquer the country, but Korea and China attracted his attention. European expansionisms in Asia awakened Japan who, in turn, also embarked on her own at the expense of her neighboring countries. During the Philippine revolution, Japan was a source of support for the Filipino revolutionary struggle. During the Filipino-American War, Japan was the only country who actively provided the Filipinos with men and arms. The 10 December 1898 Treaty of Paris where Spain ceded the Philippines blocked all foreign designs on the Philippines. However, Japan was a place of refuge for

Filipino irreconcilables. General Artemio Ricarte was foremost of them. Through these irreconcilables, Japan kept her designs on the Philippines alive.

The 1895–96 Sino-Japanese War and the 1905–06 Russo-Japanese War established Japan as a World Power. Victories in these wars and the rise and dominance of the military in Japan fueled Japanese expansionism. In 1928, the famous Tanaka Memorial was published. Claro M. Recto called it Japan's "Monroe Doctrine for East Asia." Anticipating the conquest of several Asian countries, the Japanese leaders drew up plans for their administration. One of them was made on 18 February 1942, entitled "Establishment of East Asia - Maneuvers for the First Period of Total War." This plan provided for a cultural program that shall effect the total de-westernization of the occupied areas. It specifically provided that inhabitants favorably disposed to Japan should be reinforced and that pro-Japanese sentiments be promoted, it being necessary for Japan's goals, especially in convincing the inhabitants of the occupied areas for the need to discard the West and embrace Japan and her "Asia for the Asians" agenda. The plan provided that the education of the inhabitants would be based on the Co-Property Sphere Plan—by re-training native teachers, sending scholars and technical personnel to and from Japan to the various occupied areas and from the occupied areas, teachers, students, leaders, etc.

were to be sent to Japan where they would be trained to serve definite roles created for them by and for Japan. Leaders, scholars and intellectuals were to be brought together to Japan to encourage the realization of the idea about East Asiatic unity. Native leaders were to be appointed to vital positions to stimulate enthusiasm of the inhabitants to cooperate and to show to them that Japan respect their traditions and beliefs. The plan also stressed that the Japanese language should be taught to make it the common language of the Co-Prosperity Sphere envisaged by the Japanese leaders.

The 18 February 1942 plan envisaged the establishment of a sphere of influence in greater East Asia with Japan as the dominant entity. And with this plan went, too, the eventual displacement of the Americans, the British, the Dutch, etc. in the areas. The de-westernization of the occupied areas was to encompass all aspects of life. All these aims were regarded as part of the first round of an expected protracted war between Japan and her enemies. When the organization of the Co-Prosperity Sphere Program was done, then the second round—the final round of the war called the "War of the Hemispheres"—would find Japan as the sole leader of the world. This would mean the realization of Japan's ultimate goal—*Hak-ku I-chiu* i.e., one world under one roof (that of Japan). "The evidence is clear," U.S. Ambassador to Japan C. Grew wrote, "the Co-Prosperity

Sphere means eventual Japanese hegemony over all the areas therein contained."

JAPANESE RE-ENGINEERING OF FILIPINO LIFE

After issuing proclamations terminating American sovereignty in the Philippines and calling on the Filipinos to cooperate, the Japanese Military Authorities banned all newspapers, and publications, radio stations, etc. except those that they converted into Japanese mouthpieces. Americans, British, and other enemy nationals were reconcentrated to prevent them from obstructing Japanese policies and "spoil the right spirit of understanding between the Japanese and the Filipinos." Their properties were sequestered and every chance were used by the Japanese to humiliate the Western nationals and held them up to the hatred and derision of the Filipinos. These were done to show to the Filipinos that white superiority over the Asians is a myth.

To effect the severance of all ties between the Philippines and the United States, all references to or about the West were removed, replaced, or renamed in Japanese or Filipino. Thus, *Kigenreki*, the Japanese calendar, replaced the Western calendar. So, 1942 became Year 2602. *Japan, Land of the Rising Sun*, etc. and other foreign names for Japan were banned. Henceforth,

Japan should be called *Nippon* or *Dai Nippon*. American names of Philippine places were also replaced. So Fort McKinley became *Sakura-heiei*, Zablan Field became *Kita-heiei*, Dewey Boulevard became *Heiwa Boulevard*, Wallace Field and Burnham Green were renamed *Plaza Bagong Pilipinas*, and Harrison Park became *Rizal Park*. Legal holidays before the war were replaced by Japanese legal holidays and anniversary dates commemorative of Japanese victories became legal holidays in the Philippines. Thus, the founding of the Japanese Empire *(Kigen-setu)*, birthday of the Japanese Emperor *(Tenyu-setu)* the veneration of Emperor Meiji *(Meiji-setu)*, the outbreak of the Pacific War, and the fall of Bataan and Corregidor were observed as holidays in the country. A new code of ethics patterned after the Japanese code of *Bushido* was enforced for all government employees to follow. The obligatory bow in the direction of Tokyo was always performed to start all public gatherings and meetings.

The cultural transformation went hand in hand with the effort to spread the Japanese language and make it the common language in the Philippines and in the Co-Prosperity Sphere. The Japanese authorities viewed the spread of their language as the "first step to bring the blessings of Japanese civilization to the less advanced peoples of Asia." Thus, Japanese language schools, such as the Nippongo Institute of the *Kan Min Ren Raku Sho*, were established not only to spread Nippongo but also to "foster closer understanding and friendship between the Imperial Forces and the Filipino people... with reference to the present and future destiny of this country."

Schools were reopened but Japanese and Tagalog languages were prescribed as the official languages and were made as compulsory subjects for all students to learn. Nippongo was made the second medium of instruction in place of English. Even in private and government correspondence, Nippongo was enjoined to be used.

EDUCATION: KEY TO THE JAPANIZATION OF THE FILIPINOS

Like the American colonial authorities four decades earlier, the Japanese authorities used education as the foundation of their efforts to transform Filipino society according to their vision. They banked on the upbringing of the Filipino youth according to their blueprint. Through them, their aim to eradicate all vestiges of Western influences in the Philippines would be realized.

Two months following their occupation of Manila, the Japanese authorities laid down the basic aims of Philippine education under Japanese rule:

1. To make the people understand the position of the Philippines as a member of the East Asia Co-Property Sphere, the true meaning of the establishment of a New Order in the Sphere and the share which the Philippines should take for the realization of the New Order, and thus to promote friendly relations between and the Philippines to the furthest extent;

2. To eradicate the old idea of the reliance upon the Western nations, especially upon the United States of America and Great Britain, and to foster a new Filipino culture based on the self-consciousness of the people as Orientals;

3. To endeavor to elevate the morals of the people, giving up over emphasis on materialism;

4. To strive for the diffusion of the Japanese language in the Philippines and to terminate the use of English in due course;

5. To put importance to the diffusion of elementary education and the promotion of vocational education;

6. To inspire the people with the spirit to love labor.

Before schools were reopened, all textbooks and other learning materials were censored of all references to Western life so that they should contain only pro-Japanese and pan-Asiatic topics. In general, only those books and learning materials that were about the Philippines, Japan, and the Orient were allowed to be printed and circulated. A Textbook Examining Committee was created for this purpose.

The elementary level was given priority in the reopening of schools. The Japanese authorities stressed that the elementary pupils "will best bear the imprint of the New Spirit—being the forces of the policy of intellectual readjustment for the Philippines." Since love of labor was to be emphasized, normal and vocational schools as well as those of the natural sciences (such as agriculture, medicine, and engineering) were given priority. Private schools were allowed to reopen one year later.

Educators, school teachers, and educational leaders of the Philippines were brought into frequent meetings with the Japanese authorities in calculating in them their task to emphasize the above educational policies. They were also retrained in the various institutes established by the Japanese to install in them the policies pertaining to the place of the Philippines in the New Order of East Asia and the role the Philippines would play.

The elder Filipino generations were not spared in these cultural transformations. A Government Employees Training Institute was created to provide training for government employees in performing their duties under Japan's New Order. A New Life Camp for Young Filipinos and Japanese was established in Balara, Quezon City, to show that Filipinos and Japanese could live together harmoniously, thus providing a symbol of Asian solidarity. A training school was established for Constabulary officers who would shoulder the burden of keeping domestic peace and order for the Japanese Military Administration. An Institute for Former USAFFE soldiers was established where ex-USAFFEs, before they were released from confinement,were subjected to a series of re-education programs capped by a mass oath-taking of loyalty and adherence to Japan. There was also established a Naval Technical Training School for Filipino boys for service in the Japanese navy yards. A Cultural Institute of Tagaytay was established where young Filipinos were sent to imbibe the Japanese way of life and a Labor Institute for the workers, too.

The leaders of the country were also reorganized. The Japanese authorities created the KALIBAPI (Kapisanan sa Paglilingkod sa Bagong Pilipinas). Its by-laws enumerated its functions—to ensure a stable foundation for the New Philippines; assist the people in knowing the importance of, and strengthen their adherence to, the principles of the Greater East Asia Co-Prosperity Sphere; to adhere strictly to the policies of the Imperial Japanese Forces in the Philippines in their administration and to render any acts which will facilitate the reconstruction of the New Philippines and the advancement of the Greater East Asia Prosperity Sphere.

As adjuncts of the KALIBAPI, the Japanese authorities established the Junior KALIBAPI for Filipinos below 21 years old (this was later replaced by the KAPARIZ (Kabataang Pangarap ni Rizal), to be composed by all youth between the ages of six and 21. There was also the Melchora Aquino Sisterhood of the KALIBAPI and a Maria Clara Sisterhood as female counterparts.

To round up all these organizations' task to re-engineer Filipino society according to the Japanese vision, there was created the DANAS (District and Neighborhood Associations). It consisted of some ten to twenty families. Its duty was to look after the maintenance of peace and order under joint responsibility through the mutual cooperation of its member in conjunction with the Japanese Military authorities. Through the DANAS, Japanese policies were made known to the people. More importantly, it functioned as the "eyes and ears" of the Japanese authorities for the DANAS officials were enjoined to report any "stranger" in their communities and were made responsible to the military authorities.

A Philippine-Japan Cultural Relations Committee was also created to coordinate the cultural exchanges between Japanese and Filipino musicians, artists, writers, scientist, etc. A Bureau of Oriental Culture was created, tasked to study oriental culture, especially the Philippines, and its dissemination through the schools, Through the cultural exchanges, Japanese intellectuals, scholars and mentors participated in all areas of Philippine Life. Japanese athletes joined various sports activities in the country to demonstrate the idea that the Japanese people were not only intellectuals but also athletic-minded. Leading Japanese artists, musicians as well as Japanese songs were regularly featured in all radio stations. Regular concerts were held at the New Luneta by the New Philippines Symphony Society, composed of Japanese and Filipino musicians. A literary, cultural, or scholars' convention in Tokyo capped these inter-cultural exchanges.

Songwriting contests were also promoted to help spread Japan's New Order in the Philippines. On 7 February 1942, the Japanese Military Administration sponsored a songwriting contest. One of the rules of this contest stated that the "song must express the joy of the Filipinos from being liberated by their Oriental brothers, the Japanese, from Anglo-American domination as well as the spirit of cooperation with Japan in the building of a New Philippines." Later on, other themes using the Japanese policies were used such as "What I Must Do to Help the Philippines a Worthy Member of the Great East Asia Co-Prosperity Sphere," "Construction of the Greater East Asia Co-Prosperity Sphere" and, in the latter part of 1944, a contest was held on the theme "P.I. At War."

A New Philippine March was composed for the coming grant of independence by Japan to the Philippines:

AWIT SA BAGONG PILIPINAS

Tindig aking Inang Bayan,
Lahing pili sa Silangan,
Iwaksi nating ang nakaraan,
Yakapin ang bagong buhay.
Hawakan ang watawat,
Ng pagpapakasipag,
Ibandila, iwasiwas,
Ang pagbabagong-tatag.

Koro

Lakad at harapin,
Pagtatanggol sa layunin,
Hirap, sakit ay tiisin,
Upang makamit ang mithiin,
Gumawa, bumuo at magbata,
Itatag ang Silangang Asia,
Lupalop na maginhawa,
Kasaganaang sama-sama.

A New Philippine National Anthem was also composed:

PAMBANSANG AWIT NG PILIPINAS

Lupang mapalad na mutya ng Silangan
Bayang kasuyo ng sangkalikasan
Buhay at yaman ng Kapilipinuhan,
Kuha't bawi na sa banyagang kamay.
Sa iyong langit, bundok, batis, dagat na pinaglupig,
Nalibing na ang karimlan ng kahapong pagtititiis,
Sakit at luha, hirap, dusa at sumpa sa pag-amis,
Ay wala nang lahat at naligtas sa ibig maglupit.
Hayo't magdiwang, lahi kong minamahal,
Iyong watawat ang siyang tanglaw,
At sakaling ikaw ay muling pagbantaan,
Aming bangkay ang siyang hahadlang.

Over and above all the programs established by the Japanese Military Authorities to renovate Philippine life was the creation of a corps of future leaders for the Philippines among the youth of the land loyal to Japan's New Order—Filipinos thinking and acting like the Japanese—to insure the perpetuation of Japan's New Order in case Japan emerge victorious in the war against the West. Thus, just as the American authorities did some four decades before, the Japanese authorities recruited and selected young Filipinos and sent them to Japan as *Pensionados* of the Japanese Imperial Government, where they would be educated "as future leaders of various circles of the New Philippines."

SUMMING UP

The culture of the Filipino people has been re-shaped many times. From 1571 to 1898, the Filipinos were moulded to become good colonial subjects— "Cristianos"—and those who opposed Spanish rule were called by the Spaniards "salvajes," "infieles," "remontados," "bagamundos," "simarrones," etc. Press censorship was imposed and only books on or about religious topics, fairy tales, romance stories, etc. were allowed to circulate. Education thus was based on religion an the Filipinos learned how to prepare for the afterlife.

The Filipino way of life was again re-shaped when the Americans came and ruled the country. Education, too, was the foundation of their colonial policies. The aim was to make the Filipinos good citizens in order for them to be worthy to receive their independence from America. Those who opposed American rule in the country—like Macario Sakay, Julian Montalan, Felipe Salvador, Cornelio Felizardo, etc.—were called "bandits," "insurgents," "gugus," "monkeys," etc. Americanization marginalized these patriots and when World War II came, the Filipinos were well-known as "little brown Americans."

The Japanese also implemented their policies to make the Filipino people "good colonial subjects." Education was also their foundation in re-shaping Filipino society and culture. "Bakero" "Piripino roko-roko," etc. were some of the terms they used to refer to those who resisted Japanese rule in the country.

From 1571 to 1945, the Filipino people did not have the chance to shape their way of life according to their wishes or desires, the effects of the centuries of foreign rules over them prevented them from developing their culture as the other peoples did. A "damaged" culture? Aborted? One foreign observer noted that the Filipinos suffer so many "ills of the soul," foremost of these is their slavish adoration of anything foreign. Also, their lack of a sense of history, their defective education, and their attitude of being ashamed to be called "Filipino." True, these foreign rulers contributed so many good things to the country and its inhabitants. Yet, a deeper scrutiny of these effects show that many Filipinos have forgotten their own culture. Are the Filipinos a "doomed" people? Possibly. One historian wrote that the first step to destroy a people is to erase their history.

What the Japanese Military authorities did in the Philippines only show that the Philippines was but a pawn in the power struggles among powerful nations. The Philippines, actually, during World War II was not only a pawn but also a prize up for grabs for whoever emerged victorious in the conflict. Had Japan enjoyed the luxury of time, like what the Americans enjoyed before, Japan would have also succeeded in "Japanizing" the Filipinos. The MAKAPILI (Makabayang Kalipunan ng mga Pilipino) is one proof. They were composed of Filipinos who fought and died for Japan. They were the reincarnation of the Makabebes during the Filipino-American War. Viewing all these, President Jose P. Laurel, Sr.'s exhortation to his countrymen is very relevant. He said, "No foreigner can pretend to love the Filipinos more than the Filipinos themselves."

REFERENCE

JOSE P. SANTOS JAPANESE OCCUPATION COLLECTION
(Archives Division, University of the Philippines Library,
Diliman, Quezon City).

Battle for the Liberation of Manila

Prof. Jose Ma. Bonifacio Escoda

PREPARATION FOR THE BATTLE OF MANILA

Japanese military started its defense plan after the landing of American forces in Leyte on 20 October 1944. As early as December 1943 some guerrilla units were able to uncover the Japanese Military plan to make Manila a battlefield.

GENERAL DOUGLAS MACARTHUR'S PLAN

Gen. Douglas MacArthur, based on some unverified intelligence reports that the American internees would be executed, planned for the liberation of Manila, which was contrary to the strategy by other military leaders. But MacArthur's plan was approved by President Roosevelt.

There are enough proofs showing that Gen. MacArthur desired to enter Manila on 26 January, his 65th birthday.

Aside from liberating the internees at Santo Tomas, Legislative Building, and Malacañang Palace there was no other plan in entering Manila.

GENERAL DOUGLAS MACARTHUR'S PLAN

Gen. Douglas MacArthur, based on some unverified intelligence reports that the American internees would be executed, planned for the liberation of Manila, which was contrary to the strategy by other military leaders. But MacArthur's plan was approved by President Roosevelt.

AMERICAN STRATEGY

The Americans used a long but safer way to Manila by landing at Lingayen, Pangasinan, rather than the southern coast lines as expected by the Japanese.

JAPANESE DEFENSES

The landing of the American forces since the twentieth of October, 1944 made the Japanese prepare for the imminent invasion and set up massive plans for the defense of Manila, including the systematic destruction of properties and unarmed civilians and the elimination of the anti Japanese underground. Explosive charges were placed under north Manila's four bridges and other buildings. Major streets were mined. Many private buildings were confiscated and turned into outposts. Small naval guns were placed on top of several buildings. Outposts were installed in almost every major street corner manned by marines armed with machine guns.

GEN. YAMASHITA'S ORDER: RETREAT TO THE NORTH

The head of the Japanese forces in the Philippines, General Yamashita set and executed the plan of retreating to the northern part of Luzon, and declare Manila as an Open City, the orderly surrender of the strategic places to the liberators.

But before the Americans entered Manila, the authority for the defense of Manila was relegated by Lt. Gen. Yokoyama to Rear Admiral Sanji Iwabuchi, a loser of naval battles who was in Manila without any active position as castigation for a miserable and dishonorable performance in the previous naval battles.

Iwabuchi disobeyed Yamashita's order. Instead, he issued an order to make a suicidal defense of Manila with 16,000 troops. Even the Chinese and Korean clerks and cooks were trained to kill and commit suicide.

THE RUSH TO LIBERATE THE INTERNEES AT SANTO TOMAS

The 37th Infantry Division, under the Sixth Army of Maj. Gen. Krueger, of German parentage and who would disagree with MacArthur, was assigned to liberate Santo Tomas and other government buildings. Maj. General Eichelberger, a favorite general of Gen. MacArthur, knowing the prestige at stake in liberating Manila, name dropped Gen. MacArthur's, asserting that he was assigned to take part in it and laid out his strategies. Gen. MacArthur upon discovering it, just made some modifications of his pet general's plans and assigned him to attack Manila by landing from the south, using the 511th Airborne paratroopers. Maj. General Eichelberger later complained that he was not given enough intelligence reports by the other Army. A race between the two Armies to liberate Manila started.

MacArthur, due to his disappointment to the slow progress made by the 37th Infantry, called for the First Cavalry to rush to Santo Tomas. In less than a week the First Cavalry, with less than a thousand men, aboard jeeps, weapon's carrier, supported by naval planes and some light tanks of the 44th Armored Division moved with a speed never before done in history and caught up and coordinated with the 37th for the liberation of Santo Tomas. The famous Cavalry now known as the Flying

Column was divided into three groups or serials, each one with a specific task to do.

LIBERATION OF NORTHERN PART OF MANILA
MALACAÑANG SANTO TOMAS INTERNEE CAMP

In the morning of 3 February, the 511th Airborne landed at Tagaytay ridge and started moving towards Manila but were halted by Japanese forces in Parañaque.

One of the three Serials of the First Cavalry, guided by Filipino guerrillas entered Manila late afternoon through Rizal Avenue and headed towards Malacañang Palace. Meanwhile, the 37th was halted and given a heroes welcome by the jubilant population in Valenzuela, Bulacan.

The second serial under the command of Lt. Co. Hasskett Conner followed and met with the head of the Allied Intelligence Bureau in Manila Capt. Manuel Colayco and Lt. Diosdado Guytingco.

With the two Filipino guerrilla officers as their guides, the Serial after encountering some slight resistance from the Japanese outpost in Santa Cruz reached the main gates of Santo Tomas around 6 to 6:30. While Capt. Colayco was briefing Lt. Col. Conner and other Americans in the middle of the grassy island of the wide España, a grenade thrown by a Japanese sentry from Santo Tomas exploded. Capt. Colayco ws mortally wounded while Conner and other officers were slightly wounded.

The bloody battle for the liberation of Santo Tomas began. At about 8:30 three fourths of the internees at the main building, gymnasium and surrounding shanties were liberated while around two hundred at the Education building (now the hospital) were held as hostages. On the morning of 5 February they were released after successful negotiations.

The remaining Serial entered late in the evening and were met by strong and fierce resistance by the Japanese at FEU and the surrounding buildings. The street fighting or urban fighting in which the liberators were not trained for began. American casualties kept rising since. The population near the vicinity went out from their houses and jubilantly greeted the Americans.

The arrival of the Americans sent jitters to the Japanese all over Manila. People from other districts began receiving telephone calls about the arrival of the Americans and thought that in a day or two, their places would be freed at last from the savage enemy.

On 4 February the Japanese demolition squads went into action. They blew off the four bridges connecting northern Manila to the southern districts. Parts of Santa Cruz and Binondo, including the commercial and residential centers, were set on fire. The Japanese committed heinous crimes as they raped and murdered the helpless Chinese residents in the Chinatown area.

FIRST ARTILLERY DUEL IN A POPULATED CITY

The population of Manila became casualties of war as they found themselves in the middle of a deadly battlefield. The Japanese bombed UST and San Beda with the small naval guns mounted on several buildings like Saint Theresa's College in Ermita and caused some casualties. The Americans answered the Japanese artillery bombings with their own howitzers. The artillery duel which lasted for two days left several buildings and houses on fire and claimed innocent casualties as some shells fell short of their targets in Sampaloc and even in San Juan, Rizal.

On the fifth of this month the Japanese closed the gates of Intramuros, drove the people, numbering around three to five thousand, from the houses and hotels and led them to two churches. They were used as hostages for more than two weeks and started killing the hundreds of starving prisoners in Fort Santiago.

The Americans, through makeshift bridges, crossed the Pasig on the seventh and reached Pandacan and Santa Ana. They met stiff suicidal resistance in Paco and Ermita. Artillery was called to flush out the Japanese fanatical defenders. After the sporadic shelling the Japanese would get out from their raid shelters and start the systematic genocide through the use of fire, grenades, bullets and bayonets. People, regardless of age, sex, and nationality, even those belonging to the Axis countries like the Germans and Italians and neutral countries like Spain and Ireland became victims of the genocide.

On 9 February, ten Spanish members of the Vincentian order, together with several Chinese residents who were seeking refuge at the Central Seminary in San Marcelino, Ermita were bayoneted to death.

The following day, the German Club, with German residents and eight hundred people, was not respected. It was burned and refugees, including the five German nationals were killed. Women were gang raped and killed. Even children were not spared.

The following day the German, French, and Irish Christian Brothers numbering sixteen together with around forty refugees were brutally murdered inside the De La Salle College building.

As the American liberators and Filipino guerrillas inched their way through bloody room-to-room, house-to-house, and street-to-street fighting, more civilians were killed in the crossfire through the liberators, guns and bombs, and Japanese genocide tactics. Even nurses and doctors in the National Red Cross Headquarters, together with the patients and refugees were massacred.

In Ermita, the residents of the whole block from Padre Faura to Isaac Peral (United Nations Ave.) were driven away from their houses. The men were separated from the women and later killed. The women, numbering around four hundred, were led to Alhambra apartments and Bayview Hotel where they were raped by the drunken marines. Other residents were brought to Manila Hotel and Army Navy Club where they were held as hostages. Several women whom the Japanese fancied were gang-raped before they were brutally killed.

As the Americans and Filipino guerrillas encircled the Japanese positions, most of the defenders committed suicide rather than surrender. Only a few chose to give up.

Maj. Gen. Beightler wanted aerial bombardment of Intramuros. Gen. MacArthur, due to the reports that thousands of Filipinos were there in San Agustin and other places, only allowed mortar fire to enemy targets.

These mortars also claimed the lives of unaccounted civilians including one of the two attending physicians in San Agustin Church and Monastery.

On the twentieth of February, close to five hundred male residents, (almost eighty priests and Religious brothers) of Intramuros, who were starved in the warehouses near Santa Clara Convent for a week, were murdered inside the raid shelters in the lot were the Palacio del Governor once stood while the rest were machine gunned at the right side of the Manila Cathedral.

On the 23rd of February, American artillery destroyed the eastern walls of Intramuros. The Americans and Filipino guerrillas stormed and inched their way from the river bank and from Taft Avenue. The thousands of hostages held in San Agustin Church for two weeks were released but led to pass and crawl through the rubble which was in the middle of the deadly battlefield. Some were killed by Japanese snipers while others were wounded and killed by stray bullets.

The battle of Manila was over after four weeks of bloody fighting. On the third of March, the American Army declared the city free from the enemy.

Manila was in ruins and ashes. The once-proud Paris of the Orient or Pearl of the Orient was a total wasteland.

The most severely damaged were the southern districts. It was almost flattened by American howitzers and mortars. Many residents lay buried in shallow graves while the rest of the dead bodies of Japanese and civilians were scattered everywhere, in streets and ruined houses. The whole place smelled of decomposing bodies. Americans estimated that one hundred thousand unarmed civilians had perished. Sixteen thousand Japanese were killed, Americans lost 1,010 officers and men and 5,565 were wounded.

A PYRRHIC VICTORY INDEED

Among those who died in the Ermita and Malate, then the center of the social and intellectual elite, were great scientists, educators, religious leaders, priests, nuns, and political leaders.

Hundreds of thousands of intellectual property lay in ashes. The National Library lost several paintings and thousands of books. University of the Philippines lost a hundred thousand of its books and journals. Adamson lost all its books and journals and latest researches in metallurgy, electronics and chemistry to the Japanese who shipped them to Japan. Other schools who lay in ruins like Ateneo, St. Scholastica's, St. Paul, Assumption Convent, Santa Isabel, La Concordia, Letran, and La Salle suffered the same irreparable losses.

The story of the battle for the liberation of Manila which left Manila as the most destroyed Capital City in World War II, claimed by Gen. MacArthur as the "Warsaw of Asia," remains almost unknown to the rest of the world.

Paper on WWII Conference: Remembering the Past

Dr. Armand V. Fabella

PROLOGUE

If it was Beniting Legarda who made the schedule for this gathering, I hate him. He gave me one o'clock in the afternoon which is the time when all decent people should be having siestas. Now, I only have 30 minutes to talk, so let me start.

Essentially, I will talk mostly about civilian life during the Japanese Occupation from 1942 to 1945. In this connection, I think I can safely divide the audience here into two groups, those who were around during the Occupation and who perforce must now be in the pre-departure lounge, and those who were not yet born at that time. This talk of mine is primarily targeted at the latter, who was not yet around then, and who cannot authoritatively contradict my impressions now.

First of all, I have seen the assigned topics, and I want to announce right now that I don't want to complicate the other more exciting themes in this conference.

Second, I would like to break down the Japanese Occupation into three distinct periods. The first period is from the beginning of the war on 8 December 1941 until the fall of the Philippines, or more specifically until the fall of Corregidor in May 1942. The second is the period from the fall of the Philippines until the first American air raids over Manila in September 1944. The third is the period following, until the end of the Pacific war in August 1945. I mention these periods because I want to zero in on the middle portion. The middle portion was after the Filipino and American forces had surrendered, and ended the euphoria of a "thousand-mile-long" convoy coming to the rescue. The third period was when the American planes began appearing again with unfamiliar blue-and-white insignia and people began saying "Aba, may mangyayari ata." The middle period, however, could be characterized as the period of survival and despondency.

Third, I should refine further what I should be talking about. There have been a number of histories about the Philippines during the period of the Japanese Occupation. All of them I think have their strengths and their shortcomings. But before I read them, I would like to recall a famous statement by the Foreign Secretary of the United Kingdom, who said at the beginning of World War I that "One by one the lights are going out all over Europe. I do not think we shall see them lit again during our lifetime." I think that's a fairly good idea of the feelings of the Filipinos at that time when the war broke out. They began with a sense of misplaced euphoria and went on to two years of despair roughly from the second half of 1942 to the first half of 1944. Well, this is truly a reflection of life during the Japanese Occupation.

The last point that I want to make beforehand is to say that mine are mostly remembered experiences, and not necessarily the most important events. They are mostly reminiscences because there was an insulting phrase in the "Death of the Philippine Nation," saying, "we want to hear from those who are still around."

THE BEGINNING: IRRATIONAL EXHUBERANCE (1941–1942)

Let me start of by talking about the preparations for and the early days of the war. I will only make two comments about the things I remember.

The first is that just before the war, it was very fashionable to design and construct air raid shelters. At that time, an air raid shelter whether outside the house or inside the house, poured with cement or whatever or dug in from the ground, was a sure-fire topic of conversation. I mention that because that is something I never forgot. We were remodeling and extending our house in Mandaluyong; the house was built of wood but the extension was poured and reinforced concrete including the roof, serving as a real air-raid shelter. One felt relatively safe when the Japanese began bombing Intramuros and Nichols Field right after the war started, and the whole house would shake.

The second one was the fact that, when occupation of Manila by the Japanese appeared inevitable at the onset of the New Year and Manila had been declared an "open city," the American merchants opened their *bodegas* and warehouses in the Port Area, full of goodies in preparation for the Christmas season. You had all the tinned food such as ham, salmon, and mackerel, and cigarettes, among others. Rather than having the stocks fall into Japanese hands, the warehouses were thrown open to the general public to take what they could, and it could hardly be called "looting." Now, if you went into the *bodegas* to take what you could, you would be fighting with a lot of other people with the same thing in mind, but if you waited outside and bought whatever was being taken out by the cartons, you would have more time and you could even select. My father waited a respectful distance outside the warehouses, and as the people would go back and forth with cases and cases of food, he would buy them cheap. The resulting bonanza kept us going for a while. By the way, when the Japanese entered Manila, the first thing they did was to padlock the *bodegas* of Liggett and Myers, the tobacco people who were the distributor of American cigarettes. I mentioned that because the second part was when life began to be a little more difficult, and then much more difficult.

I ask myself: What were those characteristics which had to do directly with the military part of the Japanese Occupation? The one which was the most memorable for me was the house-to-house searches. The Japanese soldiers would go to your house without any warning and begin to search. What are they searching for? I don't know, but I do remember when they searched our house, one of the soldiers took a fancy to our typewriter and took it away in his jacket. Later on, the captain in charge came by to see how things were going on, and my father who had spent some time in Tokyo when he was still a bachelor spoke to him in Japanese. The captain seemed impressed, ordered the typewriter returned, and then he turned to the soldier who had taken the typewriter and slapped him hard on his face in front of us. I remember that.

Another Occupation policy was the prohibition on listening to shortwave broadcasts, with the death penalty for disobedience. So, we had to take all our radios with shortwave capabilities to someplace where they removed the short-wave parts and they would return it to you. You could still listen to KZRH which later became PIAM or "Putang Ina Ang Makinig." However, after the electronic surgery apparently it was very simple to recondition the radio so that you could listen to San Francisco and station KGEI, which gave us news from time to time, aside from KZRH.

A third event which surfaced after the fall of Bataan and the Death March was the formation of the Young Ladies Association of Charity, or YLAC, which began life providing assistance to the Filipinos still in prison camps in Capas. I have four cousins in O'Donnell, and three of them died later of natural causes. The fourth is still hanging on and I keep telling him to let us have his memoirs. The only problem is that in his memoirs, "siya siyempre ang bida."

THE MIDDLE GAME: DESPONDENCY AND DESPAIR
(1942–1944)

Now, let me come to the period, when I remember, which is what I call this period of depression and despair, from the middle of 1942 until the middle of 1944. The first I remember were the movies shown during the wartime. Things were not all bad. I remember the excitement I felt which came with the showing of the first Japanese film "Hawaii, Malay Sea Battles," about the Japanese attack on Pearl Harbor, followed by the Japanese attack on the British battleships off Singapore soon afterwards. The second interesting movie was a joint Filipino-Japanese film titled "Dawn of Freedom" with either Leopoldo Salcedo or Rogelio de la Rosa, and in any case I found it very entertaining. The one I remember most vividly was a movie called "The Five Scouts," which was very well done, about Japanese soldiers on patrol in China. I did not know until long after the war that it was directed by Akira Kurosawa, and it was the first movie that came out where he was acclaimed.

So that's one medium with the penetration of Japanese culture into daily life. The second had to do with certain songs which up to the present time I still remember. I don't know how many of you can still sing "Miyoto o-ka-i no sora akete..." I never learned to speak Japanese until long after the war, and I never went to school during the war, but I remember the words. This was part of the things ingrained into us as children.

The second musical piece was not a name, but it was a song called "Radio Taiso," to the music of which you had to do group exercises every day to this music coming from the radio.

The third entertainment medium is related to the second and had to do with what at that time we call vaudeville (*bodabil*). As we ran out of heavily censored pre-war Western films, which the Filipinos were familiar with, there was a resurgence of the stage show. Originally, it filled up what was originally a sort of little space between the showings of the movies, and then later on, it became the only feature. That was where among other things I learned this song, "Kung ang nais mo ay ligaya sa buhay, sa libis ng nayon doon manirahan," and so on, and so on, and so on. I don't know how many times I heard that. That was an example of vaudeville.

Finally, as another medium of communication and culture, we had some interesting new publications. How many of the pre-departure people here remember something called *Shinseki*? *Shinseki* was a Japanese publication during the war extolling the Japanese way, and it was something distributed widely. There was also a book published in Manila by a Japanese about the war in Bataan, from their point of view, of course, titled "The Flowering of Racial Spirit," which zeroed in on a soldier who had plucked out one eye in the battlefield and after the action was over went back to look for his lost eye. Really heady stuff.

The last aspect of the Occupation which has always remained vivid (to a twelve-year old, anyway) was the fact that you had to bow low in front of any Japanese sentry. Whenever you pass a sentry, you bowed. Not the way a cabinet member might bow to our President, but really bow and bow low. I remember I tried to avoid the sentry at the Dasmariñas bridge, behind the Escolta, so I took the long way around. Bam, bam, bam, there was another sentry there; you could not win. The sentry business was associated with faceslapping, which the Japanese considered a relatively mild form of rebuke, but to us, it was very demeaning. So, you begin to get some idea, those of you who were not born then, about life at that time.

Now, we come to the hardships. The first section I gave was what I called the Japanese Informers. The second was more a question of hardships. The first hardship that we should remember was the introduction of what we call a Japanese script. I did not know its name, nor did I come across the term "Mickey Mouse" money until after the war. During the war, I don't recall having heard it called

Mickey Mouse, but the fact is, with the introduction of a limitless Japanese-issued currency, it was only a matter of time before prices began to escalate.

The memorable problem was the rice shortage. The rice shortage was not a shortage all over the Philippines, but it was a shortage of rice coming into Manila. It lasted for two years, from 1943–44, and it was compounded by a terrible catastrophe which I have never seen since then, what we called the "Baha" of 1943. Those of you who are familiar with Mandaluyong may remember a crossing between General Kalentong and Pasig (now Shaw) Boulevard. In a large flood, the water would go as far as the knees and maybe the waist, but during the Baha of November 1943, the water rose above the heads of persons. It was a very bad flood which lasted for four days, and as a result rice was wiped out, and prices began their terrific jumps after that.

There was already at the same time two types of thinking about the future of Japanese script. One group felt that even though it was Japanese money, they were sure that any future government would honor Japanese-printed script. The other and more skeptical group felt that the *Mickey Mouse* money would be worthless in the future, and therefore you should avoid hanging on to Japanese script. If you make money, it would not be worth much in the future, and therefore you should exchange it for some thing with more lasting value—such as jewelry. You put it in jewelry because no matter what happens, the value of those jewels would remain, and you could always sell it. Others put it in real estate, but the worry remained that any real estate transaction during the war might not be honored later. So we had problems of choice. But nevertheless, never put it in currency.

Another aspect of the Occupation had to do with the disappearance of canned goods and preserved goods. All you were left with were dried fish and fresh foods which you could pick up from the market. Tinned foods from the Philippines were not being produced. Now, remember, this was only Manila. During the Occupation, by the entry of the Japanese, there was relatively little damage is done outside Manila. Whereas when the Americans came back, the damage was all over the country. It was a different thing entirely.

Now, I will give you the names of a few plants. It did not take long for me to develop a strong dislike for them. One was talinum, cooked with mongo beans. Another was *malunggay*, cooked with mongo beans. A third was *talbus ng kamote*, also cooked with mongo beans. The fourth was *kangkong*, again cooked with mongo beans. These were the greens that you could grow in your backyard, eat with some rice, and that was it. In the case of rice, it was a luxury if you could eat milled rice. Normally, the rice available was what we call unmilled rice—the red rice. That was the one available—if at all. And there was a nice alternative to rice called *binatog*, made of puffed corn, freshly grated coconut, and salt. These were the common staples for Manila.

Later towards the end of the Occupation, we had a chance to live for a while in southern Luzon, and it was not that way at all. Life was relatively normal. The problems appeared to be only in Manila itself, or as the Japanese designated it, "Greater Manila."

Another development was the disappearance of the gasoline-fed vehicle. You had several alternatives. One was the development of commercial tricycles. Another was the "Dokar," which was essentially a car chassis, pulled by horses. The car would be stripped of many of its parts such as the engine and anything else to reduce weight. It would be left with the seats, and then it would be pulled by a horse. A third alternative was the so-called "Ipopi" vehicle, which was an automobile driven by a charcoal burner. You would have a little stove in the rear of the car, you would place charcoal in it, and that would provide gas vapor which could be exploded just like gasoline. If you used *ipopi*, your car would not last very long. But while it lasts, it would keep you going.

And then finally of course, imported cigarettes disappeared. It was very difficult to bring in tobacco from the north, so you began to experiment. The experiments I remember very well, because my father lived on that, were cigarettes and pipe tobacco made from dried avocado leaves which was better than papaya, at least according to my father. Other characteristics which I would not call hardships, but which were very evident, had to do with the very sharp decline in the value of the Japanese currency. And this gave rise to something called the "buy and sell." Buy and sell simply meant you would buy things and you would have two reasons, one is you're buying for the Japanese military because they needed the items like rice, and the other is you're buying it with the knowledge that in a couple of weeks, the price would have risen and you can sell it for a peso profit, not realizing that the real value of the money has also declined. The father of a friend was very much into buy and sell, and he said that the difficulty was he knew that the value of the currency would continue to decline; therefore, where would you place the profits that you made from buying and selling? That's one. The second is the fact that even in Manila there was no such thing as a unified guerrilla resistance movement. You had various armed guerrilla groups, and I still remember some. I wonder how many of these you still remember. One was ROTC Hunters; another was Anderson's guerrillas, and then there were Marking's guerrillas; the Hukbalahap;

the PQOG, the Blue Eagles, and the Chinese Wah Chi. They all hated the Japanese but at the same time, they were operating in the same turf in southern Luzon, and in many cases, they were fighting with each other. And this was only southern Luzon, without even considering central or northern Luzon for turf.

The other thing I remember vividly was the emergence of what I would call "I shall return" paraphernalia: matches and cigarettes were only part. But when they began showing issues of *Life Magazine*, brought in by American submarine, the resistance movement received a great boost: you had hard evidence of direct contact with Americans.

Since this is something we don't find anymore, are you people familiar with the *bayong*? Did you know that during the war, one very important technique for carrying intelligence documents was what we call the doublebottomed *bayong*. You would have a *bayong* and then the bottom had a second seat woven in. You would place the documents between the bottom seat and the second or false bottom, and, if you're stopped at a check point, all they could see would be the second seat. These are the things I remember.

There is a related thing and that is during one of the cases when I had the chance to look at supposed Japanese anti-aircraft installations which were being plotted in Mandaluyong (on pre-war Shell maps), I saw that to my horror, there was a mark there showing an anti-aircraft and ammunition dump located in our house. I was very patriotic: I took out an eraser and I erased the markings. When the raid came, our house was not touched.

THE END GAME: RATIONAL EXHUBERANCE (1944–1945)

The third and last period of the Occupation, as I have classified it, began with the first American air raids over Manila early in September 1944, when there was a sudden rise in our hopes, especially as you saw Japanese naval vessels being sunk just off the Luneta.

I don't know how many of you listening to PIAM (the old KZRH) noticed that every time there was an air raid, they would sign off by playing a song called "The End of a Perfect Day." Not many people noticed this but, it was done.

Another manifestation of changing times was the rapidity with which people began singing American songs which were written during the Occupation. The one I remembered most was "You'll never know," which we heard and learned from an American pilot who had been shot down.

Except for the two exceptions mentioned at the end of this paper, I have not included anything which is a problem today. All of these were problems then, but I don't think you'll find them now. All I am saying is that if you think times are hard now, it is nothing compared to what was life then. Let me close the war years with a very vivid image of rice being hauled by a truck on Divisoria. You had this boy who would dart out from behind the truck, slash a bag of rice, and disappear. As the rice grains would begin to pour out, women would suddenly appear with *walis na tingting* and *panaloks*, and they would sweep rice from the ground to their pans. It was a way of getting rice. That showed you how desperate things were. Now, if you do something like that, you will not slash it, you will simply say, "Boss, hindi ba natin puwedeng pag-usapan? Iba na, iba na." It is a different thing.

THE HERITAGE OF THE OCCUPATION

The last memory I have of the Japanese Occupation was sitting on a mountain top above Calauang town in Laguna watching the conflagration of Manila burning fiercely at night, after the fighting for Manila began in February 1945. Everything after that represented experiences in areas under Americans control, including a frightened Japanese straggler being shot dead in Bay.

I will close by dealing with the lasting heritage of the Japanese Occupation. The first was the loss on trust in the purchasing power of the Philippine peso. From a long period of monetary stability brought about by an exchange rate of two pesos to the dollar, the situation at the end where a *ganta* of rice could cost several hundred pesos represented a loss of faith in the currency, a loss which carried over long after the war.

The other thing which I consider a heritage, and this is my last point, was the emergence of defiance of the law because it was considered patriotic. It was considered patriotic to oppose government whether it be the Filipino "puppet" government, or the Japanese authorities themselves, and it is my own point of view that it served as the start of large-scale bribery and corruption. Did we have corruption before? Of course. But mostly it was something you heard about, rather than the endemic "ten percent" which now represents a rather ludicrous level of *taga*.

Beniting has arrived, and so I have to stop. Many thanks. I enjoyed discussing my reminiscences.

The Philippine War Crimes Trials, 1947–1949

Dr. Ricardo T. Jose

The post-World War II war crimes trials involving incidents in the Philippines were handled by four separate tribunals. These were the U.S. Army war crimes tribunal in Manila; the International Military Tribunal in the Far East established in Tokyo; the U.S. military tribunal in Yokohama, and the Philippine National War Crimes Office. Two were handled exclusively by the U.S. Army, one was an international court, and the last was a Filipino-run tribunal.

Japanese war criminals were charged with violations of the laws of war, such as the maltreatment of Prisoners of War (contrary to the Geneva Convention), atrocities against civilians and noncombatants (Hague Treaty). By the end of World War II, there were three identified classes of war crimes: A-class war crimes, which were crimes against peace—conspiracy to wage war, planning, preparing for the start and continuing to wage a war of aggression, or a war that violated international treaties. B-class war crimes were the so-called conventional war crimes, violations of the law or customs of war. And the C-class war crimes were crimes against humanity— murder, extermination, enslavement, deportation, and other inhumane acts committed against a civilian population (quoted in Nagai, "The Tokyo War Crimes Trial," pp. 275, 277). The authority for these was based on the Potsdam Declaration of 1945 and the Cairo Declaration of 1943, which warned the Axis powers of war crimes tribunals after the cessation of hostilities.

THE U.S. ARMY MANILA WAR CRIMES TRIBUNAL

The U.S. War Crimes Investigating Detachment in Manila had begun collecting information already before the end of the war. This was in preparation for the formal hearing of cases in Manila under the U.S. Manila War Crimes Tribunal. This was the earliest actual trial of Japanese war criminals in the Philippines, which officially started in October 1945.

Gen. Yamashita had been whisked to New Bilibid Prison in Muntinglupa right after the signing of the terms of capitulation in Baguio, preparatory to the formal filing of charges. Yamashita was the first Japanese general to be tried by a military tribunal for war crimes, and he was charged for atrocities in Manila, Batangas, Laguna, and elsewhere at the end of the war. It started on 8 October 1945, and hearings were held daily until the final judgment—death by hanging—on 4 February 1946. After last ditch efforts by his defense lawyers to review the sentence—which went all the way up to the Philippine Supreme Court and then the U.S. Supreme Court—he was executed in Los Baños on 23 February 1946. The basis for his trial—command responsibility—set a precedent and was argued for and against till this day. Some alleged victor's justice while the prosecution argued that the trial was as fair as possible.

Gen. Masaharu Homma was the second prominent Japanese to be tried by the Manila War Crimes Tribunal. He was charged with the Death March and various atrocities early in the occupation, while he was commander in chief of Japanese Army forces in the Philippines. The trial was fast, starting in December 1945 and ending on 11 February 1946. Attempts by the defense to halt the execution proved futile, and Homma was executed by firing squad, also in Los Baños, on 3 April 1946.

The U.S. Manila War Crimes Tribunal—held in the Chancery of the U.S. Embassy (the former U.S. High

Commissioner's Residence)—lasted for a year and a half, closing on 15 April 1947. It heard a total of 89 cases involving 212 persons. It meted out 69 death penalties (carried out), 33 life imprisonments; 75 fixed terms, 35 acquitted, etc.

The Manila tribunal covered B/C class war crimes, judging top generals down to privates and civilian interpreters. The generals were charged with command responsibility. Around half of the cases involved *Kempeitai* (military police); and still, other cases covered maltreatment of POWs; killings of civilians, and suspected guerrillas in guerrilla pacification operations.

Some of the cases are well known, particularly since the figures were high profile officials of the Japanese in the Philippines. Two of the four commanding officers of the 14th Area Army were tried—Yamashita and Homma. The American defense lawyers put up a fight for Yamashita and Homma, challenging the authority of the U.S. Army to try these cases and alledging victor's justice. They brought their appeals to as high as the Philippine Supreme Court, which denied that it had authority to act on the case; and the U.S. Supreme Court, which upheld the legality of the trials. However, Justice Murphy (former Governor General of the Philippines) issued a dissenting opinion which is classic in its own right and studied in law schools. Other notables included Col.

Nagahama (*Kempeitai* chief, October 1942–January 1945), and Col. Fujishige, who commanded troops in Batangas and Laguna, which carried out massacres in 1945 under his direct orders. The Cabanatuan POW camp chief was also tried, found guilty and sentenced.

The Japanese came from different prefectures of Japan (including Hiroshima) and also Taiwan. Also heard were some Celebes/Borneo cases. Atrocities investigated ranged all over the Philippines, from Luzon—Batanes, Cagayan, Laguna, Batangas; Visayas—Panay, Negros, Cebu, Leyte; Mindanao—Davao.

The U.S. War Crimes Branch, Manila, closed on 1 January 1947. but it assisted in the preparation of remaining trials until 30 April 1947. Some American lawyers continued to help the Philippine War Crimes Offices which had begun functioning by then after the Philippines became independent.

THE INTERNATIONAL MILITARY TRIBUNAL IN THE FAR EAST (IMTFE)

The IMTFE was an international tribunal in Tokyo, with all Allied countries represented. When it started hearing cases, the Philippines was not yet independent, but in the process of the trial, the Philippines became independent and sent one justice to sit on the bench, and a prosecutor to handle the Philippine phase of the trials.

The IMTFE tried Japanese A-class war criminals—those accused of conspiracy to wage war. Following the footsteps of the Nuremberg Trial, political, military and economic leaders of Japan such as former Prime Minister Tojo, Admirals Shimada and Nagano, foreign ministers Togo and Shigemitsu were tried. Directly related to the Philippines was Gen. Akira Muto, who had been Yamashita's Chief of staff but had also been involved in pre-war planning and operations in China.

Justice Jaranilla sat for the Philippines once it became independent in 1946. Another Filipino, Pedro Lopez, was a member of the International Prosecution Section and presented the Philippine case, which included the massacres in Manila, the Bataan Death March, inhuman treatment to POWs and others. A number of witnesses from the Philippines were brought to Tokyo to testify.

Twenty eight persons were charged in all as A-class war criminals of which seven death sentences, 16 life terms, two fixed terms, three acquittals were handed down. The trials lasted from 3 May 1946–29 November 1948.[1]

Muto was specially charged by Lopez for the Manila atrocities. The defense alleged that the atrocities at Manila were spontaneous and not planned, that they were a reaction to guerrillas, and that 14th Area Army did not know about it. But Muto could not deny the fact the atrocities had happened. He was found guilty of this and other charges, and sentenced to death (Muto had been in China during the Rape of Nanking).

YOKOHAMA TRIALS

The U.S. Army also held a series of trials in Yokohama, basically, B/C class war crimes and, more specifically, abuses against POWs. These trials were conducted under the auspices of the U.S. 8th Army.

Connected with Philippine atrocities was Gen. Kou Shih Yoku, a Korean general in the Imperial Japanese Army, who was commander of POW camps in the Philippines. Atrocities such as the hell ships (particularly the Oryoku Maru and the Arisan Maru), and the Palawan Massacre were committed under his watch. He was found guilty and executed.

The trials covered all theaters and not only the Philippines. They lasted from 18 December 1945 to 19 October 1949 and heard 307 cases involving 1,013 individuals, 51 death sentences, 92 life sentences, and

698 fixed terms were handed down, while 172 were acquitted or dismissed.

THE PHILIPPINE GOVERNMENT WAR TRIALS

Very little is known about the trials of suspected Japanese war criminals by the Philippine government. The Philippines became independent on 4 July 1946, and the Philippine government took over responsibility over those cases which the Americans had not finished, and which involved Japanese atrocities perpetuated against Filipinos. It carried out its own war crimes trials fom 1947 to 1949. This part of the paper will examine the highlights of the trials conducted by the Philippine military tribunals, trials which were conducted by Filipinos, their outcome and impact.

President Sergio Osmeña established a National War Crimes Office (NWCO) to function under the Judge Advocate General of the Philippine Army on 16 August 1945, a day after Japan capitulated to the Allies. This office was to work with the U.S. National War Crimes Office, also in the Philippines, to speedily carry out the just punishment of Japanese war criminals "guilty of atrocities, cruelties, and acts of oppression against the people and armed forces of the Phihppines, and the citizens of other member of the United Nations." No specific courts were created by this order, but the NWCO functioned independently of, but in close collaboration with, the U.S. Army in compiling data relating to atrocities and assisting in the prosecution of Japanese in the U.S. war crimes trials in Manila.[2]

In the Philippine Army, a War Crimes Division was formed, headed by Maj. Fred Ruiz Castro, which also investigated Japanese atrocities.[3]

After independence, a new NWCO was created on 29 July 1947, by President Manuel A. Roxas to carry out "the speedy trial of all Japanese accused of war crimes committed in the Philippines," including those who had planned or helped plan the war of aggression and those who had violated "the laws and customs of war," murdered, plundered, wantonly destroyed, exterminated, and enslaved the people, among others.[4] Maj. Eleuterio P. Fojas succeeded Castro as the head of the new NWCO. Fojas had been a prosecutor during the American phase of the trials and had been successful in some of them.[5]

The U.S. Army had handled all cases of war crimes in the Philippines from the end of the war until the Philippines became independent, as per the Cairo Declaration of November 1943, which stated that war criminals would be judged "by the people they have outraged" and also pursuant to the Potsdam Declaration of July 1945. Unfinished cases were then transferred to the Philippine government to handle. The Philippine government did not have the machinery to handle such cases in 1946, and the U.S. military tribunals continued to handle cases until 29 July 1947, when the NWCO was formally created. With the creation of the NWCO, the Philippines took over all remaining war crimes cases from the Americans.[6]

The new NWCO was tasked not only with investigating and prosecuting these war crimes, but also in establishing military commissions, which would try the cases. It was independent of the U.S., but would maintain close liaison with the Legal Section, General Headquarters, Supreme Commander of the Allied Powers in Japan. The NWCO would use the Articles of War, which had been adopted by the Philippine Commonwealth government in 1938, buttressed by the Rules of Land Warfare as published in U.S. manuals and as recognized in international law.

The NWCO functioned under the Philippine Armed Forces' Judge Advocate General's Office Lt. Col. Fred Ruiz Castro, a Bataan veteran and head of the first NWCO. He was named Judge Advocate General in 1946, a post he retained until 1953. The chief of the NWCO was Maj. Eleuterio P. Fojas, who served in this post until June 1948, when the Assistant Chief and Executive Officer, Capt. Mariano A. Yenko, Jr., took over. Administrative

Officer was German S. Wambangco, and Chief of the Prosecution Division was Capt. N. Maronilla-Seva. Chief of the Defense Division was Capt. Pedro Serran.

The military commission's rules and regulations were patterned after the U.S. Army practice. Each commission had, in addition to the military judges and the prosecution and defense panels, a legal member, a professional lawyer and military officer to decide on legal issues. The prosecution was handled by Philippine Army regular and reserve legal specialists. The members of a military commission was appointed by the President of the Philippines or such person delegated by the president. Strict qualifications were set so that the members would not be influenced by personal prejudices and interests. As much as possible, the heads of the courts corresponded with the ranks of the accused: thus in the trials of Japanese generals, Filipino generals were appointed to the commission; in the case of Admiral Takesue Furuse, the highest-ranking Filipino naval officer, Commodore Jose V. Andrada, was named head of the military commission. In cases where the trial involved incidents which the commission members might have been privy to, the defense could and did ask the Filipino officers to inhibit themselves—which they did. As an example, in the case against Yoshio Tsuneyoshi, Capas Prisoner of War Camp Commandant, the legal member, Capt. Lorenzo Camins voluntarily inhibited himself after the defense asked if any member of the commission had been in Capas.

The defense panels were initially composed of Japanese, two lawyers per defendant. But when several irritants occurred, the Japanese were removed. These irritants were attempts to cause delays in the trials (probably in the hope that a formal peace treaty would be signed which would remove the legal basis for the Philippine National War Crimes Office). The Japanese asked for postponements for even minor reasons, causing undue delay. The Chief Prosecutor, Capt. N. Maronilla-Seva, went to the head of the Japanese defense staff—composed of lawyers from Tokyo—to complain in December 1947. As he stated his case, he was attacked from behind and thrown on the floor by one of the Japanese defense lawyers. One of the Japanese interpreters joined in and tried to kick Capt. Maronilla-Seva, while other lawyers pinned him down. A scuffle ensued, which was resolved by NWCO officers and employees.[7]

After this incident, the Philippine government removed all the Japanese from the defense panel and created an all-Filipino defense team instead with only one Japanese representative from Tokyo.

The head of the Philippine panel for the defense was Capt. Pedro Serran, who had been a staff officers in the guerrilla resistance movement in Panay. Although he knew first-hand about the Japanese atrocities in Panay, his commitment to justice and fair play transcended his own personal feelings. When asked about his views, he said: "I am not concerned with securing the acquittal of these Japs, but to assure them a fair trial. That is what we fought for in the war: democratic justice, due process of law—even for the Japs."[8]

Other members of the defense panel included Capts. Jose G. Lucban and Artemio Alejo, professional lawyers but also officers in the Philippine Army. They carried the defense in the big cases with distinction—and without bias, even though the job was unpopular and seen by some as the end of their law careers.[9]

After the verdict was issued, it still was subject to examination by the Board of Review for the Commanding General, Philippine Army, after which it was passed on to the Office of the Secretary of Justice, representing the President of the Philippines, for review. In exceptional cases, the president himself could review the verdict and sentence.

CONDUCT OF THE TRIALS AND MAJOR CASES

The NWCO attempted to strictly follow the rights of and proper procedure for the defendants, which included receiving a copy of the charges and specifications; representation by counsel; the right to testify on his behalf and present evidence for his defense; the right to have all materials translated; the right to a preliminary investigation; public hearings; and the right to have competent justices. In short, strict enforcement of due process would be followed as far as practicable. This was criticized by some as being in favor of the Japanese, who themselves did not follow due process during the war. Despite this public sentiment, the NWCO tried to keep the trials above board.

The NWCO handled 73 cases involving 338 Japanese, from lieutenant general and vice admiral to privates and civilians. (Chaen chart says 72 cases, 169 individuals). Many cases involved massacres but in same cases there were few witnesses, and the lack of evidence led to their closure. Another problem was lack of positive identification. Many of the commissions were strict on positive identification of the perpetrator; when such was lacking, cases could be dropped. Further problems involved the lack of funds and transportation to bring witnesses to Manila from the provinces. Also, many of the perspective witnesses were breadwinners and could not be away from their families for a prolonged period of time. Without witnesses or sure identification, there could be no case.[10]

Where there were witnesses, another problem was that some became very emotional and tried to get their hands on the accused. They had to be restrained and the law allowed to take its course.

The NWCO immediately went to work and, within one month, had started actual trials. By January 1948, twelve cases had been tried, with six finished. The first cases to be tried and completed included that of Chushiro Kudo, the "Butcher of Bay." His trial was begun on 25 August 1947, and ended just more than two months later, with the first sentence promulgated by a Filipino military tribunal sitting on the war crimes cases: death by hanging. The second case, held from 23 September to 3 December, was that of Sadakichi Takahashi, which also resulted in a sentence of death by hanging. The fourth case heard—Yoshiaki Kodama—resulted in a twelve-year prison term; Takefumi Fujita got a life sentence; Saburo Fujisaki, twenty years. Many of these were identified as perpetrators of massacres or else were *Kempeitai* (military police) officers.

Where the prison sentences were to be served was unresolved at that point: with Japan still under Allied occupation, the convicted war criminals were held in the New Bilibid Prison in Muntinlupa, just outside Manila. With the signing of a peace treaty with Japan, however, it was probable that the sentences would be served in Sugamo Prison in Japan, where it was believed the Japanese would set them free. Philippine prison officials recommended that the Japanese convicts serve their whole sentence in the Philippines.[11]

Some of the cases lasted for months. Among the longest was that of Gen. Shigenori Kuroda, who had been Commanding General of the Japanese occupation forces from 1943 to 1944. Kuroda raised the question of the legality of the NWCO to try his case—since Congress should have passed a law creating it, rather than Roxas' executive order. The shortest case was that of Vice-Admiral Takesue, who pleaded guilty on the first day. The trial lasted just three days. Also short was the trial of Maj. Tsuneyoshi, Capas camp commander, had already been tried and sentenced in Yokohama.

The cases can be grouped into four specific types: 1) high ranking officers with command responsibility, whose cases usually had several specifications in the charge, such as maltreatment of Prisoners of War, massacres and tortures; 2) cases involving *Kempeitai* officers and enlisted men, who carried out smaller, localized killings and tortures; 3) perpetrators of massacres of civilians or suspected guerrillas in guerrilla pacification campaigns; and 4) specific cases such as, for example, the case of Jose Abad Santos' execution in 1942; the maltreatment of POWs in Camp O'Donnell in Capas, and cannibalism in Mindanao.

The most senior Japanese officers tried were lieutenant generals. One was Lt. Gen. Kuroda, whose case lasted for six months and was divided into an American phase and a Filipino phase. He was charged with killings and maltreatment, which occurred under his command. Many witnesses were presented, but in the end his lack of attention to his duty (he was known as the playboy general during the war and played golf rather than inspect the defenses) saved him from the death sentence. Even before the trials finished, he challenged the legality of the tribunal in the Philippine Supreme Court, but this was turned down. He was given a sentence of life under hard labor. He maintained his innocence, however, and even after the verdict was handed down, continued to fight for his case. He was eventually given a special pardon in 1951.[12]

Lt. Gen. Shizuo Yokoyama, commander of the Shimbu Group, whose command included the Manila area and southern Luzon, in which many massacres had taken place, had been directly under Yamashita. He was judged guilty and sentenced to death by firing squad.

Another ranking officer tried was Lt. Gen. Kiyotake Kawaguchi, who was charged with the murder of Jose Abad Santos in 1942. Together with him in this case was Maj. Gen. Yoshihide Hayashi, Director General of the Japanese Military Administration in 1942. Contradictory testimonies of the two as to who was responsible for the fateful orders led to Kawaguchi taking his defense and pleading guilty for the killing, but not guilty for issuing the order. For this, and the efforts of his defense panel, Kawaguchi was given a fixed prison term (six years). Hayashi, because he did not tell the truth and consistently denied everything Kawaguchi stated, continually claimed innocence and ignorance of the order, was sentenced to life.

Adm. Takesue Furuse, who had been involved in the Battle of Manila but was specifically accused of massacres conducted by his men in Infanta, Tayabas (Quezon) in 1945, was the highest ranking Japanese Navy officer tried by the Filipino courts. Furuse pleaded guilty at the outset of his trial, despite warnings of the consequences by the tribunal. Even the prosecution had to ask him if he was sure. Before the court issued its verdict, Furuse announced to the court: "If death should be given me, I hope my death will be like oil poured on the troubled sea that represents the affairs of these nations. If my fate is life, I shall dedicate the rest of my life to the atonement of my errors." The verdict was guilty, the sentence death.

Several of those tried were *Kempeitai* officers and men. Lt. Col. Hideichi Matsuzaki, had saved Elpidio Quirino (Vice President at the time of the trials) from arrest and torture, was aided by a personal letter by Quirino in Matsuzaki's behalf to confirm that it was Matsuzaki who saved him in Fort Santiago. But, due to other killings and brutal treatment elsewhere in the Philippines, he was meted life.

Others who were tried were pre-war Japanese residents of the Philippines, who had joined the occupying Japanese forces as interpreters, agents and aides in torture and executions.

The last case heard was that of Maj. Gen. Kenshichi Masuoka, chief of the *Kempeitai* in Baguio. The trial ended in late 1949, and the last decision of the Filipino war crimes trials was ten years hard labor. After this, the NWCO, its mission accomplished, closed down in March 1950. The tribunals lasted for almost two and a half years, from 1 August 1947 to 28 December 1949 (Chaen, "U.S. Trials," 242).

It is of interest to note who was not tried: Adm. Denshichi Okochi, commanding the navy forces in the Philippines; Lt. Gen. Takeji Wachi. Director-General of the JMA and deputy chief of staff of the 14th Army, and Gen. Akira Nara, commanding the 65th Brigade, which perpetrated killings in the Bataan Death March, the Pantingan river massacre, and anti-guerrilla operations. Murata, Okochi, and 14th Area Army staff officer Shujiro Kobayashi, however, testified in the Tokyo trials in Muto's defense.

PROBLEMS AND ISSUES

Various problems faced the tribunals. One was the difficulty of obtaining witnesses for the trials. Among the legal issues were the constitutionality of the commissions, the absence of citations of specific violations of law, command responsibility, the problem of having to carry out illegal orders, the admissibility of evidence such as affidavits and others. A serious problem was also the difficulty of identifying specific perpetrators, as most massacre victims were not in a position to know the names of the Japanese.

Many Japanese accused the Philippine trials of being a vendetta, where Filipinos pointed to any Japanese just to get even. Misidentification of names, of units was a constant problem. Filipinos were not familiar with Japanese names and sometimes gave other names, usually of those Japanese who could speak some English. But some of this was also caused by the Japanese themselves, as some used false names, gave false locations of their units and so on just to save their necks. Some of them were able to escape conviction and were even sent home, with the result that another Japanese was left holding the bag. It appears that there was lying on both sides. It was extremely difficult to get the truth, especially with the limited time, budget, and difficult domestic problems. One Japanese wrote: "U.S. forces did relatively correct trials. But after the Philippines became independent and our trials were transferred to the Philippine side, the trials had become completely absurd and unfair and I was convicted with the death penalty" (But this Japanese himself lied when he was interviewed years later). Some perpetrators were able to get away; others could not be tried because they had died in battle.[13]

Executions were carried out even as the trials went on: the first to be executed was Chushiro Kudo, the "Butcher of Bay," in August 1948. This was followed by two in November 1948, Tsukiji Teramoto and Shizuo Nakano, in November 1948.

The Japanese government, echoing public sentiment in Japan, ceaselessly requested the repatriation of the accused Japanese war criminals. Japanese who had befriended Filipinos before the war joined in the move, contacting their Filipino friends to hasten the process. Some Filipinos, in Congress or elsewhere, supported their Japanese friends' calls.[14]

Most Japanese did not see the Japanese war criminals as real criminals and saw them as victims—even martyrs—of the war. Many appeals were made on their behalf, and the continued trials and executions hindered the re-establishment of normal relations between the Philippines and Japan. The plight of the Japanese war criminals was heightened when a song was composed by two of them and recorded in Japan by the popular singer Hamako Watanabe. The resulting song, "The Night Goes on in Muntinglupa" became a sentimental hit in Japan and furthered the call for their release.[15]

Sometime after the last execution in 1951, the appeal of a Japanese woman member of the Upper House of the Japanese Diet was published in a local periodical, urging President Quirino to order a retrial and to wait some months before carrying out the next execution. To her, the Japanese war criminals were not criminals, as they had simply followed higher orders. She appealed to Filipinos to write Quirino and other leaders to reconsider the trial verdicts. But the Japanese legislator failed to consider the Filipino sentiment for justice and the hatred still burning from the unresolved issues and the sense of loss. Many Filipinos responded negatively to her appeal and refuted her claim that the accused were not war criminals, as they had enthusiastically carried out orders or more. The incident showed the gap in perceptions between the Japanese and the Filipinos:

the Japanese thought that the Japanese could never have committed crimes on their own and should be granted clemency while the Filipinos sought justice and retribution for losses caused by Japanese operations and atrocities.[16]

Not all Filipinos understood the need to be fair to the Japanese. Some wanted to kill any Japanese in revenge for the atrocities and killings they had committed. The Filipino defense panels received letters from irate Filipinos in the provinces, criticizing the Filipino defense panel as pro-Japanese.[17]

Although the memories of the war were still clear, the Filipino defense lawyers took their job seriously and ably defended their wards, to the consternation and criticism of the people at large. There was no shortage of Filipinos who wanted to hang the Japanese convicts, but the Philippine government and the Filipino defense panel wanted to show the world that the Philippines could carry out impartial trials.[18]

A minority of Filipinos criticized the trials as victor's justice or vengeance, not dissimilar from the Japanese methods during the war. However, others criticized the slowness of the courts and their seeming bias to the Japanese.[19]

The convicted war criminals were kept in Muntinglupa. Seventeen of the death sentences were carried out: the first in August 1948; two in November 1948, and the rest in January 1951.[20]

The convicts were treated humanely, and the press was allowed to interview them. Japanese Buddhist monks were allowed to visit, as well as Christian missionaries. Some of the prisoners were repentant; others insisted on their innocence; others emphasized that the Filipinos they killed were spies or guerrillas and not ordinary civilians. None of them complained of ill-treatment in prison. Some of the Japanese accused were changed by their experience: some became Christians, while others became strongly Buddhist. At least one stated if executed, he hoped it would serve as a lesson against war, and if allowed to live, that he would dedicate the rest of his life to peace. A few even volunteered to help the Philippine government fight the Huks, who were then fighting against the government.[21]

Because of the good treatment they were given by Muntinglupa Prison Superintendent Alfredo Bunye, a special bond between the Bunye family and the Japanese developed, which continued to this day.

THE RELEASE OF THE CONVICTED WAR CRIMINALS

In February 1951, President Elpidio Quirino pardoned one Japanese military officer who had been sentenced to 20 years hard labor, provided he never return to the Philippines. Gen. Kuroda was released in 1952, just before a Japanese reparation mission (the Tsushima Mission) visited the Philippines.

Two years later, effective 4 July 1953, Quirino granted special pardon to prisoners with jail terms, and commuted death penalties to life imprisonment. All remaining terms would be continued in Japan, and all convicted Japanese war criminals were returned to Japan that year on condition that they never return to the Philippines.

The decision was "motivated by humanitarian motives and the fostering of early restoration of normal ties between the Philippines and Japan." The Japanese were sentenced to either definite prison terms (27), life imprisonment (31) or death (56). They would be delivered to the Japanese government and would serve their sentences in Sugamo Prison.

A few months later, in December 1953 in one of his last acts as president, Quirino gave all Japanese convicts a special amnesty, thus ending the war crimes trials phase of the Philippine-Japan relationship.[22]

The timing of these releases can be lined with the signing of the San Francisco Peace Treaty; with growing U.S. pressure for the Philippines to abandon reparations claims in light of Cold War developments and the need for a friendly Japan. It can also be connected with the failure of the Japanese to acknowledge responsibility for the war and their unwillingness to pay reparations.

Quirino was criticized by his opponents, who had hoped to use the war criminals as a bargaining chip for reparations. Politicians belonging to the rival Nacionalista Party believed that the Philippine position had been weakened by the release. On the other hand, it did pass the ball to the Japanese court and gave the Japanese: the next move in the deadlocked reparations talks. Still, Quirino's public explanations—he did not want his children to inherit the hatred in others' hearts, especially since the Philippines and Japan were neighbors and nothing could change that; it was the Christian thing to do, and so on—remained a difficult pill for Filipinos to understand and accept.[23]

SUMMARY OUTCOME AND FEATURES

STATISTICS[24]

	U.S. PHASE (1945–1947)	PHILIPPINE PHASE
No. of cases tried	88	73
Total number of defendants	216	338
Sentences		
Death by hanging	70	71
Death by musketry	9	8
Life imprisonment	36	31
Fixed items	74	27
Sentences disapproved	3	1
Acquittals	12	13
Cleared	-	187
Not tried	9	-
Cases dismissed	-	3

The Filipino courts emphasized fair play—even despite the loss of the Japanese defense panel. Why? The Philippines was a newly-independent country, and wanted to show the world that despite the popular anti-Japanese feeling, it was capable of conducting fair trials. The Philippine government did not want to host a kangaroo court, and wanted to keep the process strictly within legal limits. Even after the incident involving the mauling of the chief Filipino prosecutor, the Philippine government appointed Filipino defense panel with one

Japanese. One journalist noted that despite the strong anti-Japanese sentiment of the country, the Philippine government bent over backward to give the Japanese representation.[25]

The Philippine government spent time and money to ensure a fair, judicially sound trial, as opposed to trials elsewhere, to show that the Philippines was a responsible member of the international family of nations. It recognized the probability of being accused of carrying out the victor's justice and tried to keep the proceedings proper. There were failures along the way, but many of the trials were indeed handled responsibly.[26]

The trials were conducted at a time when the Philippines faced severe economic dislocation as a result of the war and the Huk rebellion (in which dissidents were often killed by forces and were not given justice—unlike the Japanese). Ironically, the Japanese were given the benefit of the lawful process while the Huks were not.

As other more pressing problems developed, amidst the threat of a new war, interest in the war crimes trials receded. But the anger in many Filipinos remained for several more years. The Philippine War Crimes Trials Program was an attempt to prove that despite this anger, the government could still maintain a balanced view in terms of international justice, and towards Japan.

NOTES

[1]   The most thorough coverage of the Filipino participation in the Tokyo Trials is by Hitoshi Nagai, "The Tokyo War Crimes Trial," 261–298 in Ikehata Setsuho and Yu-Jose, Lydia (eds) *Philippines-Japan Relations* (Quezon City: Ateneo de Manila University Press, 2003).

[2]   Executive Order No. 64, *Official Gazette*, (41:6 September 1945), 414–415.

[3]   Castro later became Judge Advocate General of the Armed Forces of the Philippines and still later rose to become Chief Justice of the Supreme Court Victor J. Sevilla, *Justices of the Supreme Court of the Philippines, Volume III* (Quezon City: New Day, 1985), 14; Teodoro M. Locsin, "Day of Reckoning," *Philippines Free Press*, 17 January 1948, 35.

[4]   Executive Order No. 68, *Official Gazette* (43:9 September 1947), 3547–3553. Roxas' authority to create this organization was challenged by Gen. Kuroda's defense lawyers, who claimed the war crimes program should have been established by law.

[5]   Such as the case against Col. Yamaguchi, commander of the Japanese forces in Negros Occidental; Yamaguchi was judged guilty and was hanged).

[6]   Guillermo S. Santos, "The War Crimes Program of the Philippines," *Philippine Armed Forces Journal*, (IV:2 January–February 1951), 29–31; Locsin, "Day of Reckoning," 18–19.

[7]   Locsin, "Day of Reckoning," 19.

8   Locsin, "Day of Reckoning," 18.

9   Artemio Alejo interview; Lucban article in *Shuroku Ruson*. Despite losing some of their cases, the Japanese defendants were very impressive and were full of respect for the Filipino defense lawyers.

10   Locsin, "Day of Reckoning," 34.

11   Locsin, "Day of Reckoning," 34.

12   Enrique B. Santos, "Conquerors No More," *This Week*, 3 December 1950, 11.

13   Jintaro Ishida, *The Remains of War: Apology and Forgiveness* (Quezon City: Megabooks Company, 2001),212. This particular Japanese said executions were carried out every Friday, which scared the accused war criminals— but actually they were only carried out only three times, and not all were on Friday.

14   Lydia Yu-Jose, "Philippine-Japan Relations: The Revolutionary Years and a Century Hence," in Aileen San Pablo-Baviera, and Lydia Yu-Jose, (eds.) *Philippine External Relations: A Centennial Vista* (Manila: Foreign Service Institute, 1998), 312.

15   Kiyoshi Osawa, *The Japanese Community in the Philippines Before, During and After the War*, (Manila: Joshu Bunko Library, 1994), 235–236. NHK did a documentary on this, shown last August, during the annual anniversary of the end of the war. Quirino was given a copy of the record, and some Japanese believe it moved him to release the accused Japanese in 1953.

16 "Letter from Japan," "FP Readers Reject Appeal for Jap Prisoners; Mrs. Kora and her Appeal," *Philippines Free Press*, 5 May, 26 May, and 9 June 1951; Yu-Jose, 611–312.

17 Artemio Alejo interview.

18 Executive Order No. 68; Piccigallo, 188–191; Locsin, "Day of Reckoning," pp. 18–19, 34; Irene P. Bueno and Luis S. Balanon, "Let Me Hang Them!" *Philippines Free Press*, 28 February 1948, 44–45.

19 Santos, "The War Crimes Program of the Philippines," 29–31; Philip R. Piccigallo, *The Japanese on Trial: Allied War Crimes Operations in the East, 1945–1951* (Austin: University of Texas, 1979), 195–196; Adamin Tallow, *Command Responsibility* (Manila: privately printed, 1965), 201.

20 *Evening News*, 4 July 1953; Yoshio Chaen, *BC Kyu Sempan Firipin Saiban Shiryo* (Tokyo: Fuji Shuppan, 1987). The last execution was carried out just before Allen Dulles visited the Philippines in a bid to get the Philippine government to accept the proposed Japanese peace treaty, in which reparations would be waived.

21 Piccigallo, 194; Santos, "Conquerors No More," 9–12.

22 Yu-Jose, 312; *Official Gazette*, Vol. 47, No. 2, 2 February 1951, xiv and 49; 47:12 December 1953, clxxxv; "Forgiving Neighbor," *Time*, 27 July 53, 15.

23 Yu-Jose, 312; Takushi Ohno, *War Reparations and Peace Settlement: Philippine-Japan Relations, 1945–1956* (Manila: Solidaridad Publishing House, 1986), 85.

24 Santos, "The War Crimes Program of the Philippines," 27.

25 Locsin, "Day of Reckoning" and Santos, "The War Crimes Program of the Philippines" cite this.

26 For claims of injustice, see Ishida, Remains of War. Ishida balances these claims with Filipino views of the courts.

Hiroshima and Us

F. Sionil Jose

Some thirty years ago or so, I was in Kawazaki near Tokyo attending a conference sponsored by the Afro-Asian Writers Union—a Moscow-supported organization. During the first plenary session, an Indian communist took the floor and started lambasting the United States for dropping the atom bomb on Hiroshima and Nagasaki. He made it appear that the Japanese were the tragic victims of World War II.

I was so infuriated, I rose from my seat and shouted, "Mr. Singh, your country was never occupied by the Japanese Imperial Army! When the atom bomb was dropped on Hiroshima, and Nagasaki, I called the Americans ninnies for they did not atomize Tokyo, Osaka, Kyoto—in fact, all of Japan. This nation deserved to be atom bombed for the atrocities it committed in my country."

That weekend, all the delegates were invited to Kyoto; only my wife and I were excluded from that tour.

We mark this week, the 60th anniversary of the Japanese surrender. I am not sorry at all—through this span of years—for the atomic bombing of Hiroshima and Nagasaki; I just pray though that such holocaust will never visit any nation in the future.

Those who condemn now the atomic bombing of these two cities, do so out of the context of those times, ignorant as they are of the feelings of people ravaged by the Japanese Imperial Army.

There was no moral barrier when these cities were bombed—it was total war, a response to the Japanese rape of Nanking in China, to the leveling of Coventry in England by the Nazis and the extermination of the Jews, the massacres in Ermita-Malate and elsewhere in the Philippines. No, I will never, ever weep over Nagasaki and Hiroshima.

And if any strategic justification is needed, both Hiroshima and Nagasaki were major staging areas for the Japanese Army. The bombings forced Emperor Hirohito to end the war thereby saving millions of both American and Japanese lives. Just remember that the Japanese were prepared to die for their homeland with every man, woman and child; their suicidal stand in Okinawa was a grim foreboding of what would have transpired if those bombs were not dropped.

I was a high school senior in 1941 when Pearl Harbor was attacked but before that attack, war clouds already hovered over Asia. Japan had occupied French Indochina, half of China and Manchuria. Close to us in the North. Formosa was already in Japanese hands. Chunks of Davao were Japanese abaca plantations that produced hemp for the Japanese navy and maritime industry. Douglas MacArthur, retired, had come to the Philippines to help set an Army of 21-year-olds and Camp O'Donnell in Capas, Tarlac where the recruits trained—would later become the notorious prison camp of the survivors of Bataan.

Air raid, blackout, and evacuation drills were held in Manila. All of these, however, proved useless when the war finally came.

The Japanese planes bombed the first Nichols airbase near Manila, Fort Stotsenberg in Pampanga, and the airbase in Iba, Zambales. MacArthur had an eight-hour warning of the debacle at Pearl but the U.S. Air force was caught on the ground.

Classes were stopped. I went home to Rosales, Pangasinan, and was there when the Japanese arrived. They came in bicycles, open trucks, and like most Filipinos at that time, I thought they would not last, that the Americans would come in a massive convoy and drive the Japanese back to their homeland. After all, through all those years, we didn't expect them to produce those airplanes and battleships. We knew that Japanese products were shoddy and easily broken. Made in Japan was inferior. We were, of course, sadly mistaken.

The miles and miles of convoy did not arrive, Bataan then Corregidor fell.

The first weeks of occupation in my hometown were quite correct. The Japanese distributed rice, textiles, then, their true nature surfaced. They started slapping and beating up people for the slightest infractions. By the second year, supplies, particularly medicines and food became scarce. We had to do with ersatz products, *castanog* (roasted coconut meat), charcoal fed engines, *talinum* and *camote* gardens even in the islands of the streets. Towards the end of the Occupation, the poorest Filipinos wore sackcloth. Without rubber and leather, fancy wooden shoes became fashionable.

I commuted between Manila and Pangasinan, bringing rice to my relatives in Manila. The buy and sell business flourished. Divisoria in Manila the center. In June of 1944, I enrolled in preparatory medicine at the University of Santo Tomas, walking every morning from Antipolo Street near Blumentritt all the way to Intramuros. The streetcars still ran but they were extremely crowded.

The rich had *dollars*—fancy *calesas*, drawn by retired racehorses. Only the Japanese and their powerful puppets had cars.

One morning, while we were having Niponggo lessons, suddenly the anti-aircraft guns atop San Juan de Letran College nearby started popping, then grey stubby planes with a white star and bars roared over Intramuros. Some flew so low, their canopies open, we could see the pilots waving. Americans! The whole class started jumping, shouting, shrieking. Our instructor—a young Japanese officer with his sword on his side always—slinked away.

Classes were permanently stopped and that afternoon, at around two, the second wave came, so many planes darkened the sky. Anti-aircraft guns spat at them, their black puffs dotting the sky, but not a single plane was shot down. When they came again the following day, the anti-aircraft guns were silent.

By this time, there was already very little food in the city. Even gutter rats were trapped and eaten. We stayed on for another month, then in early November, my mother, a cousin, and I left Manila with a small bag of rice, a cooking pot, and some dried fish. We walked to Pangasinan for seven days.

The highway was deserted in the daytime but for people like us fleeing the starving city. American planes from Leyte ranged the plains, the highways, blasting bridges and trucks—we came across one burning in Angeles, the dead Japanese in it. At night, we slept under empty houses around the highway—their inhabitants have fled to the interior and at night, we could hear the Japanese marching, retreating.

In early January 1945, the Americans finally returned to Luzon. From that distance in Rosales, we could hear the big guns off Lingayen as battleships pounded the beaches for the landing. That was a terrible waste for the Japanese had all left.

When the Americans got to Rosales, at the first opportunity, I joined a medical unit of the Combat Engineers. I had one ambition—to go to Japan with the invasion and once there, first chance I get, I will kill as many Japanese as I can.

That was sixty years ago, and thinking back, this is how I truly felt and, I'm sure, so did many others, particularly those who lost their loved ones to Japanese villainy. It embarrasses me to recall this objective—a result of my witnessing what they did and in a way, what they did to me certainly, is nothing compared to those who survived Fort Santiago, and the torture sessions with their *Kempeitai*.

Collateral damage—some blame the Americans for the destruction of Ermita, Malate, and Intramuros and the death of thousands there. But the Japanese were there, raping, burning, killing. If they were not killed, what would have happened? Was there ever a less violent alternative?

We can get sentimental and nostalgic over history in mind and we must restore Intramuros as a reminder of our past and as a tourist attraction. But we must also never forget that Intramuros was the seat of a colonial power that shackled us for three centuries, just as Ermita-Malate—and the beautiful antiseptic Makati today—was the seat of domestic imperialism which keeps us poor.

Many aspects of that three-year Occupation need to be studied more for they reveal so much of the Filipino character, of the myriad reasons why this society has evolved into what it is now, almost rudderless, without any lasting memory and therefore, without a sense of nation—this, despite the heroic sacrifice of many Filipinos. After all, while much of the region succumbed easily to Japanese blandishments and power, we Filipinos fought them tenaciously, valiantly.

But in that guerrilla war, for instance, all too often the guerrillas were not only fighting the Japanese—they were also fighting each other over turf, over leadership. Perhaps as many Filipinos were killed by the guerrillas, as by the Japanese.

It is the height of irony that the best organized and the most courageous guerrilla group who fought the Japanese—the Hukbalahap—was demonized almost immediately after World War II, to preserve the hold of the landlords and their American allies on government.

The Occupation showed how the peasants in such adversity, could survive and thrive, and as the Huks had abundantly shown, the peasants could also fight and win. If at all, the Occupation strengthened the grassroots movement, infused iron into the peasant's backbone and his liberation could, perhaps, be this blighted nation's hope as well.

Developments such as these cannot be quantified—they can only be perceived.

For a brief period during the Occupation, Filipinos also got to know a bit more about Japanese culture, What an accomplished people, they are and, most of all, how they modernized their country in just one generation by adopting Western technology but never abandoning their Japaneseness.

And finally, the issue of collaboration, not just with the Japanese, but with all the colonizers who ravaged this nation.

In looking at this issue, perhaps, it is also time that we attended to one man whose unique position in our history is clouded by controversy and misinterpretation.

I am now very clear in my understanding of Artemio Ricarte, the Ilokano general who was one of the leaders of the 1896 revolution. He had refused to pledge allegiance to the United States after the defeat of the ragtag revolutionary army. Steadfast in his refusal to accept American rule, he eventually fled into exile in Japan from 1911 until his return to the Philippines with the Japanese in 1941.

He was not given a high position by his Japanese friends. He was too old then—late seventies—but he served them particularly in their pacification campaign.

When the Japanese retreated from Baguio deep into the Cordilleras in 1945, Ricarte went with them. Without his knowing that the Japanese executed some 20 of his relatives as the Japanese feared that his relatives knew too much. His own grandson, Besulmino, would have been executed, too, had he not understood what the Japanese were saying and he pleaded with them to spare his life.

Ricarte had no choice but join the Japanese. He was afraid of the guerrillas who were by then better armed with the continuous arrival of aid from the Americans.

In Funduang, in Ifugao, he was afflicted with dysentry. With very little to eat, he fell ill and died. I was able to interview one of the Japanese civilians who was with him to the very end. His aide wrote a book about Ricarte titled *Even the Devil Will Weep*—for that, indeed, was the tragedy of this Filipino revolutionary and patriot whose undoing was his stubbornness, and his dependence on a foreign power.

Ricarte, teaches us one important lesson—a nationalist revolution must never, never seek outside assistance in ideology as well as in resources. It must triumph with its native genius and sinews.

The political ramifications of collaboration with the Japanese extended into the political life and destiny of the nation. Those who collaborated with the Japanese,

Claro M. Recto, for instance, were instrumental in developing a postwar inward-looking nationalism that was virulently anti-American, much to our disadvantage. We had a foot in the door to the vast United States market, a market which was exploited by Korea, Japan, Taiwan. We didn't exploit it. Imprisoned by the Americans in Iwahig for his collaboration with the Japanese, Recto vowed never to let the Americans forget what they did, claiming that Roxas collaborated more than him.

At the very least, those who collaborated with the Japanese were granted amnesty by Roxas. But those who collaborated with Marcos, who helped him plunder this nation are now openly in power without an amnesty from the Filipino people.

What else should we remember of the Occupation? It exacerbated our moral decline. During that period, all rules were thrown out and it was each man for himself. So much of this attitude remains even after the invader had left.

Our elites had collaborated with whoever ruled—the Spaniards, the Japanese, the Americans, and Marcos. As a political issue, collaboration with the Japanese died when Jose Laurel, the Japanese puppet president, got elected to the Senate. But as a moral issue, collaboration still rankles, and because we have not collectively denounced and punished those collaborators, does this mean then that we are not a moral people?

There is such a huge gap between being eighteen and being eighty. Today, I now have several Japanese friends and I value their friendship We do not talk about World War II, about Hiroshima—they know how I feel. But while we do not talk, this does not mean that we will forget. Many Japanese feel guilty over their country's past, many do not approve Prime Minister Koizumi's visits to Yasukuni Shrine which honors their war dead, including some war criminals. This issue has no consensus in Japan although it is evident that the swing towards rationalizing and justifying that war is gaining ground.

Life must go on and our future, which is bleak, indeed demands our intelligent attention, our hindsight.

In 1905, Japan defeated Russia and emerged from that war as a Pacific power with vaulting nationalist confidence to embark on an expansion into Korea, Manchuria, China, then the Greater Co-Prosperity Sphere.

A hundred years later, today, in 2005, we see the emergence of China, rivaling not just Japan but America.

In 1955, the American scholar Theodore Friend wrote a book *Between Two Empires*—that is us—the Philippines—caught between America and Japan. In that book, he concluded: "Could the Philippines accomplish the work of economic diversification and social and cultural unification, necessary to make a national community out of an ex-colony? How long would the Philippines remain in confusion, between two civilizations inherent and emergent, as well as in peril with two empires—Chinese and America?"

In our relations with China, we must not forget that we have a small but powerful Chinese minority that controls 80% of the economy, who are in manufacturing, trade, banking, media, shipping—you name it.

These Taipans came to the Philippines very poor, as all immigrants from China were. Through their industry, cunning, and exploitation of elite politics, they build profitable conglomerates, then remit billions made in this country to China, billions that should have stayed here to build industries so our women don't have to go abroad as housemaids and prostitutes.

There is an old Asian saying that when elephants quarrel, the grass gets trampled. A corollary to that is, when the elephants make peace, the grass gets eaten.

But this, perhaps, is the subject for another conference.

The German Community in Manila During the Japanese Occupation, 1942–1945

Edgar Krohn, Jr.

At 7:49 a.m. on Sunday, 7th December 1941 (8th December in Manila) the Imperial Japanese Navy launched an aerial attack on Pearl Harbor, the American naval base situated in Hawaii.

The news came as a shock but, it must be said, not unexpected. War had now come to our shores. What many had feared would come, had now become a reality.

Very soon, Manilans would experience their first baptism of fire when at about three a.m. of the following day,

9th December, the city came under attack by Japanese Aircraft. We were awakened by the crunching sounds of bombs exploding in the not too far-off distance— Nichols Field in Pasay. The huge siren installed atop the Philippine cold store building opposite the Metropolitan Theater, commenced wailing, announcing that an air attack was in progress. Search light rays stabbed into the darkness of the skies and cracks of anti-aircraft guns contributed to the lights and sounds of battle.

At the time, my father, mother, and I were living in a spacious compound in Pasay which contained six houses, all of which were occupied by German nationals, with the exception of the largest one. There resided the proprietor of the property, who was a German naturalized Filipino citizen.

Totally unaware of the dangers of an air raid, the residents of all the houses spilled out into the garden to watch the spectacle that had unfolded in the sky. How little did we know of the dangers from falling anti-aircraft shell fragments that could maim and kill. How much we had yet to learn about aerial and ground warfare, for later in the morning, numerous pieces of such fragments were found in various corners of the garden.

During the succeeding days, the members of the German community were filled with anxiety and great concern over the future. They were certain that it was but a matter of time before the United States and Germany would be at war with each other. Three days later, 11ᵗʰ December, at midnight, Manila time, the Germans, listening to radio Berlin, heard Hitler declare war against the United States. The die had been cast. The agonizing wait was over.

On 12ᵗʰ December, the U.S. Army commenced to take male Germans into custody for internment. I recall the incident quite clearly. It was towards noon when a Meralco bus pulled up and parked alongside the street where we lived. An American officer followed by six or seven Filipino soldiers in full battle gear and wearing steel helmets emerged from the bus and proceeded towards the nearest house in the compound. Some of the soldiers took up defensive positions behind trees and seemed to be covering the officer and his escort of one or two soldiers. They appeared to be fresh recruits— perhaps ROTC—as they were quite nervous. In the house, the officer ordered that all German males were to report immediately so that they could be transported to an internment camp, the location of which was not disclosed. After checking his list, the Officer commanded everyone to board the bus, which then drove off.

It was only some five days later when we learned that they had been brought to Muntinlupa to a detention camp identified as "Enemy Alien Concentration Camp," which, not too long after, was re-named "Camp Muntinglupa." It was a barbed-wire enclosure located just outside of the wall of the new Bilibid Prison which had been constructed in 1935.

Within this area of confinement, which held approximately 300 Japanese nationals, 72 Germans, and a small number of Italians, stood some two-storied barracks made of sawali. Access to the second floor was through a small round hole from which was affixed a ladder. The buildings have built-in double deck bunks and nothing more. There were no interior toilet facilities. Latrines, showers and washing facilities were all located outside of these buildings. The internees were kept in the barracks at night and were not even allowed to go to the latrine. The windows had no glass, only wooden shutters and they were kept closed at night, making the barracks quite hot and uncomfortable. No lights were permitted at night and the doors were padlocked. After a few days these intolerable conditions were fortunately relaxed. Windows could be left open at night, blackout lights were installed in the barracks and whenever an internee had to answer a call of nature, he would position himself beside the locked door and shout: "Guard, shit!" and the guard would escort him to the latrine.

Upon arrival of the internees at the camp, they were listed after which they were relieved of their personal effects. Toilet articles and cigarettes, which were later returned to the internees, money, fountain pens, mechanical pencils and the like were inserted into envelopes, sealed and dropped into a large box. Aside from the toilet articles and cigarettes, the other confiscated items were never seen again. No bedding or mosquito nets and no mess kits were issued to the internees. From discarded tin cans, the Germans fashioned drinking cups and small plates from their use. At the outset, the meals served to them were prepared by the Japanese internees who were confined in the adjacent compound. It was, in the words of one of the internees, just plain lousy. Things, fortunately, took a definite turn for the better when a group of Germans and Italians volunteered for kitchen work. A German former chief steward aboard the pre-war inter-island vessel, *Mayon*, was appointed steward of the mess, while an Italian cook was assigned to prepare all the meals for the Germans and Italians. Dishes, utensils, mess tables, and chairs were also obtained through the American Camp commander. And so, conditions improved considerably. It must be mentioned that, while the American officers were at times overbearing and arrogant, the Filipino guards and their officers did what they could within their means to ease some of these unpleasant conditions.

On Christmas eve, some of the wives of the internees brought some cheer into the lives of their husbands when they went to the camp, bringing with them gifts and even a Christmas tree.

On Saturday, 27th December, my mother and I, together with other ladies and children, drove some 20 kilometers of gravel roads to Muntinglupa. It must be remembered that Muntinlupa was, at that time, very sparsely populated. A trip thereto from Manila was, at this time, not without risks as the Japanese invaders had by then already seized control of the air space not only over Manila but over the entire island of Luzon. Our trip was, fortunately, not interrupted by the appearance of unfriendly aircraft. It was indeed a joyous occasion to see my father again. He informed us that there were rumors circulating in the camp that they would be released the following day as the Japanese forces were rapidly advancing towards Manila. It was not a rumor, as the next day the internees were told they were free to go.

During the evening hours of 2 January 1942, the Japanese troops occupied Manila in an orderly and disciplined manner and quickly restored order in the chaotic city, a city that had degenerated into a state of disorder and lawlessness. This anarchic state of affairs developed after the American authorities opened the warehouses in the piers and encouraged the people to take what they wanted to prevent the stored goods from falling into the hands of the enemy. After the warehouse, had been emptied, the mob proceeded to loot the Japanese bazaars in Escolta and Quiapo areas, and from there the rampage spread rapidly and indiscriminately to the Chinese sari-sari stores and other smaller establishments. The police were completely helpless and did not have the capability to restore order, because when Manila was declared an open city and the military withdrew its forces from Manila, the law enforcement personnel were disarmed in compliance with the requisites of declaring Manila an open city.

On the following day the released German internees and their families gathered together at the the German Club for a thanksgiving and fellowship lunch. It would be appropriate here to mention something about social clubs. During the early decades of the 20th century, social clubs of foreign nations played a significant role in their lives. These clubs were small corners of their homeland where they could enjoy the company and fellowship of their fellow countrymen, relish the dishes of their native lands, make use of the libraries stocked with books and periodicals from their motherland. These clubs had their recreation facilities such as bowling alleys, tennis courts, billiard tables. Their national holidays were always celebrated in a very festive manner and were always looked forward to by the cosmopolitan residents. The Germans had their Deutsche Klub, the Spaniards their Casino Español. The Britons had their Manila Club, which even possessed its soccer field. There was also the Nippon Club as well as the Swiss Club, while the Americans could enjoy the facilities of the University Club, the Elks Club and the Army and Navy Club. More so during the time of the occupation would the German Club become the center of interest and activity to its nationals. The German spirit of cohesiveness and cooperation and their willingness to help each other especially in these demanding times, would ever so often come to the forefront. For recreation, bowling, chess, and card game tournaments were organized. Low-cost luncheons were served for the benefit of its members. In deference to the war, the festive Oktoberfest and Fashingsfest *(mardi gras)* were not held, only the traditional Erntedankfest—harvest-thanksgiving day was commemorated ceremoniously. The very dynamic and dedicated club president, Max Kummer, was successful in his efforts to obtain from the Japanese military administration, three privileges for the German Club.

One was a monthly beer ration for its members from the San Miguel Brewery which was, needless to say, greatly appreciated.

Second was a permit to install a short wave radio receiver, under certain restrictions, to enable the members to listen to broadcast from Germany. Once or twice a week, the German news agency would broadcast short personal greetings and messages from persons who had relatives residing in countries in East and Southeast Asia. On such evenings, many members would gather around the radio set and anxiously wait for their names to be called and to hear some news from their loved ones in the homeland. Each message beamed to the Philippines was carefully recorded by a stenographer, so that those who were not in attendance could be duly notified in the event a message for them had come over the airwaves. Such evenings were also occasions for the members to stay on for dinner and to socialize with their friends.

The third was that the Japanese authorities granted a permit to the German Benevolent Society to operate a Jitney, which was similar in configuration to our today's jeepney. This vehicle was to be used for emergency purposes and also to transport foodstuffs for the benefit of the community. During the middle part of 1944, when food items became difficult to come by, the club established a store, located in the garage, where these foodstuffs, purchased in bulk, were sold to the members at cost. With this permit came a limited monthly ration of fuel.

It should be mentioned that on 15 January 1942, the Japanese Military Administration issued an order which decreed that effective 17th January, the use of motor vehicles, except those sanctioned by the Department of Administration of the Japanese Army, would be prohibited allegedly because of shortage of gas and oil. Applications for a license to operate a motor vehicle following the list of classifications would have to be filed with the authorities. It was also decreed that the buying and selling of gasoline were prohibited. And so the only public and private conveyances available to the Manilans were the very efficiently-run Meralco streetcars, *caretelas*, *caromatas*, pedicabs, bicycles, and the privately-owned *dokar*, which was horse-drawn, often very ornately decorated, coach running on automobile tires. Seating as many as six passengers in the rear, it was entered from the back of the vehicle, just like the present-day jeepney.

In mid-1942, after the organization of the Philippine Executive Commission by the Japanese Military Administration, registration records showed that 892 German nationals were living in Manila and environs, almost equally divided into males and females.

From the outset, relations between the German community and the Japanese Military Administration were far being harmonious and with the passage of time, this situation worsened. Being aware of the reality that the Japanese, with a very few exceptions, distrusted anyone who was not of their own kind, the Germans were more or less convinced that some informers had been planted within the premises of the German Club by the *Kempeitai*, perhaps one or two of the waiters. But on the whole it can be said that the entire Filipino staff employed by the club were efficient, dedicated and loyal. Francisco, the reliable head waiter of the club for many years, was a favorite of everyone.

Caution had therefore to be observed. The restriction on limiting radio reception to radio Berlin and radio Tokyo was strictly observed, lest the member be denounced to the *Kempeitai*.

One had to be forever vigilant, especially when having conversations with friends and acquaintances in public places. If there were ever any informer installed at the club, they will surely have wondered why the word "Yapaner"—Japanese in German,was never heard in conversations between Germans. This was because when the Germans talked among themselves, the Japanese were referred to as "appenzeller." Appenzell is one of the cantons in Switzerland and perhaps, because "appen" does sound a bit like "affen," which in German means

monkeys, a wit among the members must have decided
that this would be an appropriate name for the invaders.

A mauling incident that occurred just outside of the
club premises further eroded the already strained
relationship. A Japanese non-commissioned officer
had accosted a member and had struck his face with his
sheathed sword.

At another time, a brawl erupted inside the bar of
the San Luis Hotel in Ermita, where a group of young
men of German/Spanish descent was seated at a table
enjoying each other's company with some beer. A non-
commissioned officer approached them and demanded to
know if they were Americans. He was told that they were
Germans, which did not appear to satisfy the drunken
Japanese who forcefully slapped the face of one of the
young men, who promptly stood up and introduced his
fist to the offender's face. They were all apprehended
by the Military police and hauled off to Fort Santiago,
where Mr. Kummer was later able to obtain their release.
He reasoned that all the participants were well in a state
of inebriation and, therefore, had somehow lost control
over their mental faculties. This was accepted by the
Military Police.

There were incidents where merchandise owned by a
German company was "purchased," which I would like to

put between quotation marks, by the Japanese Navy at confiscatory prices. Another German-owned company had one of its warehouses stocked with textiles sealed and taken over by the Japanese Army, allegedly that the goods were needed for the war effort. Portions of St. Scholastica's College, which was owned by the German Benedictine Sisters, were commandeered and converted into an army hospital. There were sometimes some embarrasing moments for the good Sisters, when Japanese in their G-strings would walk around the patio separating the quarters of the Sisters and the hospital.

On 26 October 1942, Bishop Wilhelm Finneman, Apostolic prefect in Mindoro, who had arrived in the Philippines from Germany in 1923, was arrested in Calapan. He had denied the Japanese Military the use of church premises and had refused to officiate a marriage between a local woman and a member of the Military Police. He was taken into custody, tortured and, after a week, taken aboard a launch and thrown overboard into the sea with weights attached onto his body. The official report of the Japanese was that Bishop Finnemann had committed suicide.

Fr. Heinz Buttenbruck possessed the gift of having a photographic mind. Because of his German citizenship, he was able to secure a special pass from the Japanese military to visit the prisoner-of-war camp at Cabanatuan for not only spiritual, but also charitable work. At the same time, he had attached himself to an underground unit and used his special talent to memorize messages, names of POWs, and other important information. He would, at times, smuggle into the camp much-needed medicines like Quinine. Eventually, his clandestine activities became known to the Japanese. Fr. Buttenbruck, the kind, and selfless person that he was were arrested, tortured, and subsequently executed.

It became known, after the war was over, that Max Kummer, president of German Club and his wife, were extending material and financial aid to POWs in Cabanatuan, through the same underground group that Fr. Buttenbruck was involved with.

Several Germans in the provinces opted to join and aid the guerrillas. One of them was Waldo Neverling. He had been on the staff of the Mindanao Mother Lode Mine and initially started in helping hide American executives, engineers, and their families from being arrested and interned. He became known as a swashbuckling hero and "pirate" against the Japanese in the southern seas with an armed launch named "So what."

In December 1942, fourteen German bachelors volunteered to depart from Manila aboard a 7,900 ton German tanker blockade breaker. The voyage of this vessel originated from Yokohama, reaching a Philippine port to load coconut oil before continuing the long and dangerous trip to German U-boat bases located in the French part of the Bay of Biscaya, when it was sighted and subsequently sunk by a British cruiser. Fortunately, there were no casualties among the Manila Germans and everyone, including the members of the crew, were rescued by a surfacing U-boat.

During the early 1943, a German military mission landed in Manila on a short stopover during the course of an inspection tour of Japanese bases in Southeast Asia. Heading the group of army, naval and airforce officers was Wolfgang von Gronau, who in 1932 had made a stop-over in Manila during his round-the-world flight on his Dornier flying boat. Von Gronau was the Luftwaffe attache at the German embassy in Tokyo. A reception was held in his and his colleagues honor at the German Club, which gave Von Gronau the opportunity to renew the friendships he had made a decade before.

At this point, it is appropriate that something should be said about the relationship between the German residents and the newly installed national socialist regime in Germany and its Nazi party. It is a fact that the instituted idealogy of the new government was alien and unacceptable to the majority of the local Germans. On the other hand, it is interesting to note that this new order of Nazi Germany found firm acceptance in the German communities in Central and South America.

Shortly after Hilter and his party seized power in 1933, an area group of the Nazi party was established in Manila. A membership drive was initiated, a drive that reaped very few recruits. This political philosophy did not sit well with the "old Asia hands," as the consulate staff called the Manila Germans. Overall, the local Nazi party had a limited number of members, perhaps less than 10% of the total number of registered german male nationals. And of these, one could say that there were only seven to eight avid and dedicated party members. The others were inactive and seemingly not too interested in the activities of the party.

In reports dispatched to Berlin at this particular time, the consulate expressed its frustrations and disappointments over the behavior and attitudes of the Manila Germans. In one of these communications, it stated that any effort on part of the consulate to apply pressures on the independently-minded Germans, which was characteristic of the East Asia German mentality, would achieve only negative effects. It was suggested that a propaganda campaign to enlighten these misguided and misinformed elements could be initiated by the Department of Foreign Affairs. The consulate was also critical over the fact that a very great number of members of the German Community still maintained friendly relationships with foreign Jews, and that they had no apparent intentions of terminating their association with such persons. Another revealing memorandum stated that "Filipinos have, at all times, looked favorably upon Germany and its people and have always maintained very friendly relations." However, having cognizance of the recent adoption of the racial laws, this discriminatory decree had caused a very disturbing effect, especially in those circumstances where Filipinas contracted marriage with Germans. This situation and the relation with the consulate of the many Germans, who married Filipinas or mestizas, had developed into a very significant problem for the new Germany in the Philippines.

Another regrettable incident that occurred was when the Nazi party organized a reception to commemorate one of the political holidays of the new Germany at the premises of the German Club. The reception line at such functions was usually graced by the presence of the area group head of the Nazi party and the president of the German Club. Invited to this particular reception were members of the American High Commissioner office, Filipino government dignitaries and officers of high rank of the U.S. Army.

The strained relations that existed at the time resulted in the refusal of both the presidents of the club and the German Chamber of Commerce to stand in the reception line with the head of the Nazi party. Those who were invited to this function, no doubt, must have taken notice of this breach of protocol.

In 1936, Gustav Sakowsky was appointed to head the consulate in Manila. He immediately initiated forceful procedures in his attempt to incorporate the club into the Nazi party. This plan failed and the traditional policy of non-political involvement observed by the club prevailed. Sakowsky's lack of success to control the membership of the club led to his resignation, declaring the club an enemy of the state. He further ordered all party members to resign from the club. Having no other choice but to comply with this order, the handful of Nazis submitted their resignations. His high-handed behavior towards the membership, including Jewish members, caught the attention of the then-American High Commissioner, who had received numerous complaints about Sakowsky's abusive posture. High Commissioner McNutt privately conferred with Sakowsky and was believed to have warned him against official interference in the activities of the German Club, which was a social organization founded in the Philippines by private German citizens, who had no political ties to the Nazi party.

It is alleged that the state department had instructed the high commissioner to advise the consulate in strong terms that it was displeased by the consul's actions in ordering members, including Jewish members of the club, to resign.

Sakowsky was, shortly thereafter, relieved of his post and was replaced by a very understanding and tactful career diplomat in the person of Dr. Lautenschlager. With the departure of Sakowsky the situation eased considerably and a period of peaceful co-existance and cooperation ensued that continued even during the occupation when the local Nazi party could have availed of the collaboration of the Japanese military administration to take oppressive actions against the Germans, Jews and people of other nationalities. No repressive acts were initiated by the local Nazi party members during the occupation, which clearly manifested where their loyalties lay.

It is interesting to note that the circle of good friends of Consul Lautenschlager did not include any zealous Nazi party members.

In July of 1941, the U.S. government ordered the closure of all German, Japanese, and Italian consulates situated in the U.S. mainland and its territories. Prior to his departure of Shanghai, the well-liked Dr.

Lautenschlager and his charming wife were honored
at a well-attended *despedida* dinner at the German
Club. Finding themselves without any diplomatic
representation, Dr. Lautenschlager had suggested that
a committee be formed composed of club members to
represent Germany's interests in the Philippines. Seven
members were elected to serve in this body, and it is
interesting to note that only three members of this
committee belonged to the Nazi party.

In early February 1944, The German Ambassador
to Tokyo, Heinrich Stahmer, arrived unexpectedly
in Manila, ostensively on an inspection. He paid
his courtesy calls on the Japanese Ambassador and
President Laurel and met with the German Community.
It was obvious that his mission was to determine who
exercised actual control over the German community—
the Third Reich or the independently-minded old Asia
Germans. He was to learn that the local Nazi leadership
was weak and that, except for a few committed party
members, the majority were members in name only.

As a consquence of this reality, the head of the Nazi
country group for Asia based in Tokyo, Otto Spahn, was
dispatched to Manila to put some order into the existing
unacceptable system. Spahn was one of the original
members of the S.A. the ruffian storm troopers of Hitler
and had arrived in Japan via U-boat from Europe in

July, 1943. He arrived in Manila by plane on 15 June, accompanied by a small group of officials. Following protocol, he paid his respect to the Japanese Ambassador and called on the minister of foreign affairs, Claro M. Recto, thereafter, he conferred in earnest with the members of the local Nazi party. He disclosed to them that he had in his possession a warrant for the arrest and deportation of Max Kummer, President of the German Club, directed to the *Kempeitai* for implementation. He made it understood, however, that the arrest could only be carried out with the prior approval of the local Nazi party. Their independent conviction and loyalty to their local fellow countryman were manifested when they unanimously voted to reject the implementation of the arrest order. Spahn accepted their decision.

His next assignment was to call a special meeting of the members of the German Club. Once convened, he read the members the Riot Act regarding the composition of the current board of directors, which did not have one single member of the Nazi party. In no uncertain terms, he strongly stated that this unacceptable situation had to be changed. An election was to be held immediately and he presented the assembly with a list of the names of candidates who, he said, were to be voted into the board. If they so wished, the incumbent directors could also participate in the election against his choice of candidates. It was hoped, he further stated, that the right candidates would be elected into office and reminded those present that everyone had relatives in the homeland.Thus he made it clear what the members had to do. I remember when my father came home that early evening. He was livid over this threat.

And so, stormtrooper Spahn was successful in changing the composition of the German Club board and returned to the land of the rising sun, which by now had started to set.

The ensuing months were increasingly difficult ones for the German community as living conditions steadily deteriorated.

In late November 1944, the German community resolved to establish two assembly points in the city to ensure their safety and to provide adequate food supplies to its members through community kitchens. This move was also undertaken, in preparation for their internment by the U.S. Army after the city was liberated from the Japanese. Those residing north of the Pasig River concentrated within the premises of the Holy Ghost College in Mendiola Street—now known as the College of the Holy Spirit. St. Scholastica's College in Pennsylvania St., now known as Leon Guinto Street, provided facilities for the Germans living south of the river.

On 3 February 1945, American forces entered Manila and liberated Sto. Tomas Internment Camp, as well as Malacañang Palace. It marked the start of a horrific, savage, and devastating battle to defeat some 12,000 Japanese defenders in Manila. The battle raged for 28 days. One hundred thousand civilians of various nationalities perished in this battle, some 70–75% of whom were victims of Japanese atrocities. The worst massacre of civilians perpetrated by the Japanese Imperial marines in the city occurred in the German Club, where it is estimated some 400 men, women and children were senselessly slaughtered by the Japanese marines. Five German nationals were among those who were killed there, while in other parts of the city, eleven Germans died from shelling or were bayoneted. Apart from these casualties, twelve German Christian brothers were slaughtered in the massacre that took place at the La Salle College.

After Liberation, 224 German men, women and children were interned by the U.S. Army at the old Bilibid Prison, on what is now C.M. Recto street. It was only on 28 September 1945, well after World War II had ended, that they were released from internment.

And so, the chapter on the occupation had come to an end, and with that, I also end this little talk. Thank you.

The Philippines in the Pacific War

Dr. Benito J. Legarda, Jr.

SALIENT EVENTS

World War II was the first—and let us hope, the last time that the Philippines was involved in a worldwide military conflict. Previously it had been fought over in wars between Spain on the one hand and the British, Dutch, Chinese corsairs, and the U.S.A, on the other hand, as well as its war for independence against Spain and the U.S.A.

In World War II, it became one of the major battlefields. Some events stand out. The biggest naval battle in history (Leyte Gulf). The biggest military surrender in American History (Bataan and Corregidor). The only Allied capital destroyed in the Pacific, and the only time in Philippine history that it was destroyed by military action. The biggest number of war casualties in Philippine history was 1.1 million. The worst massacres of Filipino civilians since the Dutch massacre of Abucay in 1647. The highest mortality in the world for prisoners of war: over 50% for Filipinos, much higher for Americans (compared to the average of 27% in the whole Pacific theatre of war and 4% in western Europe). The stopping for four months of tough veteran Japanese troops by half-trained recruits, mostly Filipinos, while all around them Allied bastions were falling like ninepins. Next only to the Rape of Nanking (Nanjing) in the number of civilians deaths in Manila.

On the 60th anniversary of the end of World War II, it may be asked if our people are conscious of these landmark events and it they are being brought out in our history courses in schools and colleges.

RESPONSIBILITY FOR DEFENSE

America, as the sovereign power, had the duty to defend the Philippines. The calamities we suffered stemmed in large part from America's military unpreparedness before the war, and its Europe-first policy during the war. At the beginning of World War II, according to Gen. Eisenhower, the U.S. Army was smaller than the Polish army.

Belatedly, in 1941 the U.S. tried to strengthen Philippine defenses. It recalled to active duty Gen. Douglas MacArthur, then under contract to the Philippine Commonwealth, only five months before the outbreak of war, and gave him command of the newly created USAFFE (United States Army Forces in the Far East), composed, it might be noted, largely of Filipinos still in training. New planes were being sent in; some were still in crates when the war started and of those which had been made operational, some still did not have the oxygen apparatus for high altitude flying.

WAR COMES TO THE PHILIPPINES

War came to the Philippine shores a few hours after the treacherous Pearl Harbor attack, on Monday, 8 December 1941, the Feast of the Immaculate Conception. People in Batanes were just going to morning mass when Japanese troops landed.

That same day disaster struck. In what has been called a second Pearl Harbor, about half the U.S. Army Air Force was destroyed on the ground at Clark Field. The planes had been flying patrol all morning but had come down for lunch. Why were they all having lunch at the same time, without staggering some combat patrols above? Warnings of the approaching Japanese planes were received from three different sources. The planes and pilots were ready to take off, but no order was given. This appears to have been a serious lapse in tactical operations for which MacArthur has been blamed, unfairly, in my view.

He had in fact ordered all 35 of the B-17s down to Del Monte in Mindanao on 1 December precisely to keep them out of Japanese range. On 4 December the order had still not been carried out, and a reminder was sent. Seventeen of the B-17s then went down, but the other 18 remained at Clark, supposedly, according to one story, because an Air Force general was giving a big party at the Manila Hotel on the evening of 7 December.

The Japanese had an initial advantage in numbers with 500 planes on Taiwan allocated to Philippine operations. Eisenhower says the Americans had 220 fighters and 35 bombers, and with the debacle at Clark, Japanese air superiority became overwhelming. Nevertheless, the remaining American and Filipino pilots put up a valiant fight, with Capt. Jesus Villamor gaining fame as an air ace, credited with downing several Japanese planes.

Cavite naval base, home of the U.S. Asiatic Fleet, was bombed heavily and repeatedly, compelling the fleet to flee from Philippine waters down to the then Dutch East Indies, where a few weeks later much of it was sunk in the disastrous Battle of the Java Sea. Java itself fell in nine days even as Bataan and Corregidor still stood firm. The U.S. Asiatic Fleet, it if was to be sunk anyway, might better have been deployed defending the Philippines, which was under the American flag.

In Manila eager young men rushed to volunteer for military duty, and long lines formed at an army station even in a light December drizzle, until an American officer came out and said, "Go home. We have no arms for you." ROTC cadets who had been quartered at their colleges were dismissed on Christmas Eve.

With half-trained and inadequately equipped troops MacArthur could not follow his (and Eisenhower's) preference for repelling the enemy on the beaches (a tactic also favored by the great German General Johannes Erwin Eugen Rommel) and, when the main invasion came through Lingayen Gulf on 22 December, had to fall back on the old War Plan Orange of withdrawing to Bataan and Corregidor. This meant a fighting retreat down Luzon's central plain, with a notable tank counter-attack at Baliuag that gained the USAFFE a little more time for the withdrawal.

OPEN CITY

In the meantime Manila had been declared an open city—Philippine army personnel, as I know from my father's experience, were given only a few hours' notice to proceed to Bataan—and the Commonwealth Government's leaders, Pres. Manuel L. Quezon and Vice Pres. Sergio Osmeña, evacuated to Corregidor where they inaugurated their new terms of office on 30 December, accompanied by only a few high officials. Before leaving Manila, Quezon had, with MacArthur's agreement, instructed the remaining officials to do everything possible to protect the civilian population short of swearing allegiance to the Japanese emperor.

Despite Manila's status as an open city (effective on 26 December), the Japanese bombed it on the two succeeding days, and produced the war's first cultural casualty, the destruction of historic Santo Domingo Church in Intramuros.

SIDE-SLIP TO BATAAN

The USAFFE's side slip into Bataan was skillfully accomplished, the over 90,000 man force remaining intact. The major deficiency was logistical; not enough supplies had been built up. Rice stocks in Tarlac and Cabanatuan could have been trucked down and were not. Some supply officers were so bureaucratic that they refused to release supplies without proper requisition papers even while retreat swirled around them. With the help of civilian volunteers supplies from Manila were barged across the bay until the last possible minute, then the warehouses in the Port Area were thrown open to the public so they could get the goods ahead of the approaching Japanese. On New Year's Eve, the Pandacan oil tanks were blown up, even as the Manila Hotel hosted a frenzied open house party.

Senior Filipino officials led by Quezon's Executive Secretary Jorge B. Vargas, who had been named mayor of Greater Manila, and senior American officials cooperated with the Japanese consul in meeting the advancing troops and arranging an orderly and peaceful entry on 2 January 1942.

In Bataan the epic struggle began. The first line of defense ran from Morong in the west to Abucay in the east, with a 3-mile gap protected by the supposedly impassable slopes of Mt. Natib. The tough and skillful Japanese troops, however, penetrated this terrain and outflanked and almost isolated the 1st regular Division, forcing it to retreat along the beaches without its heavy equipment.

LOCAL VICTORIES

The final line of defense ran across the middle of the peninsula along the Pilar-Bagac road. Initial Japanese efforts to pierce this line resulted in two Fil-American victories. One was the Battle of the Points, when Japanese attempts to land troops on the western coastal flanks of the USAFFE were repulsed and the Japanese landing parties almost totally eliminated. It was in this fighting that Japanese brutality toward prisoners became notorious.

The other was the Battle of the Pockets, when a Japanese force inserted itself between the USAFFE's I and II Corps. By now, after a few weeks of combat, the Filipinos had become hardened veterans, and the Japanese force was wiped out.

QUEZON'S EFFORT AT NEUTRALIZATION

This happened in early February. At that time Pres. Quezon, with some support from High Commissioner Francis B. Sayre and Gen. MacArthur, having in mind that American help would not be forthcoming and that Premier Tojo had announced Japan's willingness to grant the Philippines independence, proposed on 8 February to Pres. Franklin D. Roosevelt the neutralization of the Philippines and the withdrawal therefrom of both Japanese and American armies. In his reply the following day Roosevelt adverted to the Japanese record of perfidy in Korea, Manchuria and elsewhere, and said the American troops would fight to the death. He secretly authorized MacArthur to arrange for the capitulation of the Filipino elements in his forces if need be. This turned out to be unnecessary as Quezon found Roosevelt's answer "overwhelming" and undertook to abide by it. One suspects that Quezon's national pride was pricked; he could not allow Americans to sacrifice more for the defense of the Philippines than the Filipinos themselves.

The Japanese held off for nearly two months thereafter while they brought in reinforcements of men and materials. But this was merely a reprieve. America had no intention of relieving the Bataan garrison, allocating 85% of its resources to the European theatre and only 15% to the Pacific and China. Morale-boosting propaganda about mile-long convoys was exposed as a sham when Sayre, MacArthur, Quezon, and Osmeña were pulled out of Corregidor on Pres. Roosevelt's orders to prevent them from falling into enemy captivity, and flown to Australia.

SURRENDER

USAFFE morale was, of course, affected but surprisingly not shattered. With reduced rations and the spread of various diseases like malaria, it gave way only under the smashing impact on II Corps of the Japanese Good Friday offensive starting 3 April. By 9 April, Gen. Edward King surrendered Bataan, an event that plunged the inhabitants of Manila into deep gloom. Corregidor, pounded incessantly from the air and by artillery shelling, fell on 6 May.

When MacArthur left he had divided the Philippines into four commands: Manila Bay Defenses, Luzon, Visayas, and Mindanao. Washington, however, unadvisedly centralized them all under Gen. Wainwright. When he clumsily tried to surrender only the Corregidor garrison. Gen. Masaharu Homma rightly demanded in anger that he surrender all the elements of his command, and walked out on him. With thousands of captives held hostage on Corregidor, the humiliated Wainwright had to comply.

Area commanders in the Visayas, Mindanao, and northern Luzon were reluctant to accede, as some of them felt they had enough men and supplies to undertake guerrilla warfare. But the career military men faced court martial if they disobeyed. Only on 9 June was total victory declared. The surrender involved mostly American officers and a few enlisted men. Most of the Filipinos disappeared, to fight another day. But the surrender order delayed and complicated the organization of a guerrilla movement.

DEATH MARCH AND PRISON CAMP

Following the surrender on Bataan, tens of thousands of Filipinos (who formed 85% of the Bataan force) and thousands of Americans were forced to go on the brutal Death March to San Fernando, Pampanga, with a heavy toll from thirst, hunger, and bayonetting of those who were slow to keep up.

One of the worst atrocities was the Pantingan massacre when 300 to 350 Filipino officers of the 91st Division were executed with bayonets and swords. The Japanese General (Akira Nara) linked to this massacre was never prosecuted as a war criminal. Many deaths and much hardship could have been avoided if the Japanese had accepted Gen. King's offer of his vehicles to transport the prisoners. It is estimated that around 600 Americans and between 5,000 and 10,000 Filipinos perished in the Death March. Some managed to escape.

This was not yet the end. Of the approximately 54,000 who reached the O'Donnell POW camp, over 30,000 died (28,500 Filipinos and 1,650 Americans), a death rate of over 50%. Although the Philippine authorities were willing to provide food and medicines, the Japanese obstructed or discouraged such efforts.

Surviving Filipino prisoners started to be released toward the end of June 1942. The Americans, joined by those taken on Corregidor, were transferred to Cabanatuan.

CIVILIAN ADJUSTMENTS

In the meantime civilians in the occupied areas had to make drastic adjustments in their lives. They had gone from prosperous peace time to occupation by a fearsome enemy in less than a month.

The very first adjustment was to re-set their clocks an hour ahead. They were now on GEAST (Greater East Asia Standard Time). They had to learn to bow to Japanese sentries on pain of being slapped. Freedom of speech disappeared, and it was prohibited to listen to Allied short-wave broadcasts.

Within three weeks it was decreed that private cars would no longer be permitted to operate. People had to use streetcars, bicycles and horse-drawn vehicles, (*carretelas, carromatas*, and the war-inspired *dokars* using automobile wheels). Also war-inspired were surrealistic, under-powered charcoal-fed vehicles called *ipopi*. As the Occupation proceeded the streetcars started wearing out, and they became more and more crowded. With the streetcar company in Japanese hands, people regarded it as enemy property and did their best to avoid paying fares. But this surreptitious act of political defiance contributed to the erosion of ethical standards.

For the first few months imported goods continued to be sold from the stocks looted from the Port Area. But when these ran out people had to fall back on local substitutes, many of them based on coconuts. People cultivated backyard vegetable gardens, with *camote*, *kangkong*, and *talinum* as the most common items.

CULTURE AND EDUCATION

On the cultural side, cinemas had been the main form of entertainment before the war. With no new films coming in, and no local movies being made because celluloid was a war material, movie houses took to adding live programs to their movie showings. Some impromptu comedy skits satirized the hated invaders, getting the performers in trouble with the *Kempeitai*. Where the stages were not large enough there was live music that even included classical selections.

There was heightened activity in the performing arts, in plays, and even operas. At least four were performed— Cavalleria Rusticana, La Boheme, La Traviata, and Aida. The heightened activity did not however extend to symphonic music, as the Manila Symphony Orchestra avoided playing under the Japanese and although they formed the New Philippines Symphony Orchestra this gave only a few performances before fighting returned. The Japanese did send at least one musical mission from Japan in late 1943, some of whose members were very good.

In education the teaching of subjects like history was suppressed, and remaining textbooks often had pages glued over with paper to blot out passages considered unacceptable, Nippongo was compulsory and children were taught Japanese songs. The new conquerors seemed to be planning on a long occupation.

ECONOMIC CHANGES

Economically the Japanese took over all utilities and major businesses, and they initiated a program of making the Philippines complementary to Japan's war industries. Gold mining was neglected, but base metals (copper, iron, and manganese) were exploited by "high-grading," or extracting only the highest grades of ore and ignoring the lower grades, which was bad mining practice.

Sugar cultivation was discouraged, and instead cotton planting was promoted, to feed Japan's textile mills. This met with some success in Tarlac but none in Panay.

Rice cultivation was also encouraged in lieu of sugar, and this might have been a good thing for local supplies, except that it was said the Japanese took the rice away for their own troops.

Coconut oil mills and rope factories were operated to capacity as their output was useful for the war effort, and the coconut processing mills provided substitutes for imports are no longer available (e.g., margarine instead of butter). A cargo of coconut oil was even loaded on a German tanker, which was sunk by the British when already in European waters in the Bay of Biscay. Those working in these industries earned ready cash which filtered out to other occupations including the entertainment industry.

The Japanese made strenuous efforts to restore and in some cases improve transport-related facilities. The railroad was restored from La Union to Albay. Highways were repaired, although perhaps not to pre-war standards. Some of the damage to Manila's Port Area was also repaired, and small wooden vessels of between 100 and 200 tons were built in slipways along the Pasig. Inter-island shipping service was partly restored, but this was under constant threat from American submarines.

The most conspicuous improvements, because military-related, were in the airfields at Clark, Nichols, and

Nielson. They were expanded and concreted. But when fighting returned to the country transportation facilities were among the primary targets, and the repairs and improvements on docks and airfields were severely degraded.

Permeating economic life was the issuance of occupation currency, which was supposed to circulate at par with Philippine Commonwealth notes and coins. Derisively called *Mickey Mouse* money, Gresham's Law quickly took effect and bad money drove out good. Pre-war currency quickly disappeared into private hoards, aggravated by the Japanese effort to accumulate as many copper one centavo coins as possible for their war industries. The occupation currency depreciated at an accelerated pace towards the end, and it took bags *(bayong)* full of money to make purchases. In January 1945 my father recorded purchases of rice at ₱10,000 per sack from Japanese troops who were leaving our neighborhood.

Emergency notes were issued by the Commonwealth government in the early days of the war in the south, before the general surrender. Thereafter guerrilla units issued guerrilla currency by regions, provinces, and municipalities. These were very crudely designed and printed, often using recycled government blank forms.

LOCAL ADMINISTRATION

While Bataan held out it was a beacon of hope for the civilians, and even after the fall of Corregidor, most people never lost hope in an eventual Allied victory. But they realized it would be a long, dreary and difficult wait.

The next two years might be called a period of sullen resignation and impatient expectation.

It helped calm the people's fears that there was a layer of familiar officials between them and the Japanese. Pres. Quezon assured the Americans that these were not collaborators but men who were carrying out his (verbal) injunction to soften the blow of enemy occupation to the general population. They were much preferred to anyone the Japanese brought with them, like the revolutionary hero Gen. Artemio Ricarte, then all but forgotten and rightly or wrongly perceived as being too pro-Japanese. A shining example of heroism was given by Chief Justice Jose Abad Santos, who was shot by the Japanese on 2 May 1942 for refusing to collaborate. He was the only ranking Filipino official to suffer this fate.

As time went on some of the officials seemed to be collaborating a little too eagerly, and people formed their impressions about them. When their children walked along the street other children would murmur, "Pro-Jap, pro-Jap." But after the end of the war, the amnesty declared by Pres. Roxas precluded a legal ruling on who betrayed Pres. Quezon's trust and who remained loyal.

The Executive Commission under Chairman Jorge B. Vargas operated under the Authority of the Japanese Military Administration. With the Laurel Republic, inaugurated 14 October 1943, Filipino officialdom had a little more elbow room. We retrieved the symbols of our nationality—the flag and the anthem—and, although Laurel himself later wrote that the wartime republic was "powerless" and "lifeless," its ostensibly independent authority permitted a somewhat greater leeway for discretion. Laurel himself chose never to reside in Malacañang.

A close friend of the Roxas family recounts that one day Laurel visited Roxas and almost in despair said that the pressures on him were unbearable and that he wished to resign. Roxas urged him, however, to hang on because if he left the Japanese might install in his place someone more pliable.

INSTRUMENTS OF CONTROL

People carried on as best they could with their everyday lives. One of the instruments of control was the Neighborhood Association or Tonari Gumi. These associations were instrumentalities for night patrols *(ronda)*, the distribution of prime commodities (sugar, lard, soap and matches), and the recruitment of forced labor. But this service could be commuted by payment of a wage to a substitute. It was only toward the end of the Occupation that the Japanese bypassed the Tonari Gumi in the matter of labor service and forcibly picked up men off the streets.

Rice had its own distribution system, first under the NARIC (National Rice and Corn Corporation) and then under the BIBA (Bigasan Bayan). But in the capital it was a story of ever shorter supplies and ever rising prices.

Looming like a malevolent presence over people's lives was the *Kempeitai* or military police, who had the habit of picking up suspects in the dead of night for imprisonment, torture, and often death. They were assisted by secret informers and by the Makapilis, who would hide their identities by placing mat bags *(bayong)* with eyeholes and pointing out suspected guerrillas. In the battle for Manila they also helped to burn people's houses in Pasay and elsewhere. In the villages, many of them were later liquidated by vengeful townmates.

High Filipino officials had to put up with the constant presence of Japanese guards in their houses. Some of them ate with the families, but the prouder officials sent them to the kitchen to eat with the servants.

Ordinary citizens had to exercise care while talking in public. One could not speak too loudly, and people developed the habit of first looking around before speaking in case they were overheard making anti-Japanese remarks.

RESISTANCE

Even before the fall of Bataan, underground resistance began with the formation in Manila of intelligence groups and in the countryside of guerrilla organizations. These were at first uncoordinated and there were turf battles among groups with overlapping areas of operation. In the early days some guerrilla groups were little more than roving outlaw bands. Some of the better guerrilla leaders who might have infused some sobriety were caught early— Nakar, Vinzons, Adduru, Thorp, Straughn—and executed or imprisoned.

Gradually contact was established with agents landed by submarine from Australia, including air ace Jesus Villamor, and there was increasing coordination, especially in the Visayas and Mindanao. Commander Charles "Chick" Parsons was a key figure in this effort. The provision of needed medicines, supplies and arms attracted separate groups toward a more coordinated effort. Food supplies were ample in the guerrilla areas but medicines and clothing were in very short supply.

The Panay guerrillas were reported to be among the most numerous and best organized groups, with both military and political leadership (Peralta and Confessor). The Hukbalahaps were also strong and well organized, but they seemed to have difficulty coordinating with other groups. They did however take part in the Los Baños Internment Camp rescue operation.

There were different approaches to guerrilla warfare. One approach favored sabotage, ambush, and intelligence gathering, activities that would hurt the enemy but not sufficiently to provoke reprisals on the civilian population.

Another approach was to engage the enemy in combat, and this did provoke a violent reaction from the Japanese. The philosophy behind this second approach was that the reprisals would heighten the people's anger at the Japanese and make them resist more energetically.

Japanese counter-guerrilla operations often took the form of punitive expeditions, particularly in Mindanao. Japanese troops would enter an area and drive the inhabitants and guerrillas to the foothills. They would then burn houses, seize supplies and leave. The people would return to resume their daily lives, angrier at the Japanese than ever.

MORALE

It has been noted that in the period of sullen resignation and impatient expectation, most people never lost hope for an ultimate Allied victory, and this kept up civilian morale. Among the Allied internees, the same hope prevailed amid progressively worsening conditions. Most internees were confined to the University of Santo Tomas Sampaloc campus. Although food rations were skimpy, they were allowed to make purchases from vendors, and to receive various items from friends and former employees and servants. The UST internees (over 5,000) were reduced in number when 2,000 or so were transferred to Los Baños in early 1944. Privileges to older people and to members of the clergy to live outside and carry a red armband for identification were eventually revoked. A smaller group of internees was lodged at Camp Holmes in Baguio, and another in Davao.

If civilian morale, both Filipino and foreign, remained positive, the same was not true of Allied (mostly American) prisoners of war concentrated in large part in Cabanatuan. Conditions were much worse than in the internment camps. Often they were made to work hard, food rations were minimal, and medical services virtually nonexistent. Supplies gathered by charitable organizations were smuggled in by various means, and this assuaged their hardships, but the feeling of hopelessness, of having been abandoned by their country, persisted, and with good reason. Many of them would not survive the war, whether because they died of disease or malnutrition or perished on "hell ships" while en route to Japan.

One of the charitable groups that helped was the VSAC (Volunteer Social Aid Committee), composed in large part of young ladies from leading Manila families. They did not confine themselves to helping war prisoners but undertook other charitable projects. One way they raised funds was to give benefit theatrical performances featuring music, dance, and drama. Some of the VSAC girls, because they resided in Manila's upscale districts, were killed in the Battle for Manila.

UNSURRENDERED AMERICANS

Not all Americans were in POW and internment camps. About two hundred unsurrendered servicemen were in the Visayas, Palawan, and Mindanao, and they became useful once more as guerrilla operations grew.

There were also civilians on various islands, including Jesuit priests on Mindanao and Protestant missionaries in the Visayas. Although they usually stayed deep in the interior, the Japanese made some effort to reach them. Some were not too concerned, reasoning that the worst that could happen if caught would be for them to be placed in internment camps. They badly miscalculated the depths of Japanese brutality.

In December 1943, at a place they called Hopevale near the Capiz-Iloilo border, a community of Protestant missionaries and mining families fell into Japanese hands. Seventeen Americans, including eight women and three small children, were beheaded. Also killed and left unburied were countless Filipinos suspected of having helped the Americans.

In reaction to this massacre MacArthur's headquarters ordered the evacuation by submarine of as many Americans as could be gathered. From Panay alone 59 people, including a baby and two Catholic priests, were jammed aboard a submarine for Australia.

Filipinos were also victimized in innumerable and often unrecorded massacres. One such incident has been narrated by Col. Eliseo Rio *(Rays of a Setting Sun)*. In October 1943—the month of "independence"—a Japanese detachment headed for the town of Banga in Aklan. Upon learning of their approach the town mayor with some of his constituents, including women, went out to greet them, waving a large white flag. The Japanese responded to this peaceful gesture by opening fire with automatic weapons, killing almost half of the welcoming committee including the mayor. Smaller scale killings also occurred elsewhere in Aklan, as at Ibajay.

COMFORT WOMEN AND RACISM

Among those who suffered most were women forced to provide sexual services to Japanese troops, now called "comfort women." So great was their shame that they remained passive for a long time. It is only in the last few years that their cause has been taken up but they have so far received little compensation.

Japanese hypocrisy was manifested in several ways. During the early days of the Occupation, bars in Ermita and Malate advertising for hostesses would specify

"Mestizas preferred." This we were told by friends and relatives residing in the area. What I have seen personally was a bar near my father's office on R. Hidalgo St. in Quiapo with a sign reading, "For Japanese Only, Filipinos Not Allowed." This sign remained in place all through the Occupation.

COMBAT OPERATIONS

Returning to the progress of combat operations, it will be recalled that the leader of the Japanese Expeditionary Force (the 14th Army) was Gen. Masaharu Homma. He had been given 50 days to complete the conquest of the Philippines. But the resistance of the Filipino and American troops stretched this out to what Col. Uldarico Baclagon has called the 130 days of the USAFFE. After the victory parade to celebrate the fall of Corregidor, Homma went home and retired in disgrace. At his war crimes trial he would claim that he heard of the Bataan Death March only after the war.

The belated fall of Bataan and Corregidor was the culmination of the Japanese southward drive, which had scored speedy and stunning successes at very little cost, except in the Philippines. What would come next?

The answer came immediately following the fall of Corregidor, with the Battle of the Coral Sea on 7 May, when a Japanese sea borne attempt to take Port Moresby was repulsed.

The turn of the tide came at Midway four weeks later, on 4 June, when in a triumph of code-breaking the Americans learned of the Japanese plans and ambushed their carrier force, sinking all four fleet carriers (two thirds of their total) and perhaps more important, killing a good number of the best naval aviators in the world.

Overnight the Japanese were forced on the defensive. But they undertook an "offensive-defensive," pushing out cautiously from their island bastions, to make their perimeter impregnable.

They landed troops at Buna-Gona on the northeastern coast of New Guinea and started an overland drive to Port Moresby. At the same time, they began to build an airfield on Guadalcanal in the Solomons that would threaten the approaches to Australia.

They also tried unsuccessfully to land on Milne Bay at the easternmost tip of New Guinea. They got within 20 miles of Port Moresby after weeks of hard fighting but they were turned back and driven to the coast after more weeks of hard fighting and heavy losses.

Meanwhile, in August, American marines landed on Guadalcanal and seized the nearly finished airfield. The Japanese had erred in pushing out beyond the protection of land-based aircraft. In a six-month slugging match, they won some brilliant tactical naval victories but also lost some, and were never able to tilt the strategic balance as the U.S. marines fiercely defended their newly-won airfield.

When these battles ended early in 1943, the Japanese were definitely on the defensive. MacArthur said, "No more Bunas" meaning no more frontal assaults. He would start leap-frogging over Japanese strongholds on the New Guinea coast. He was helped by the use of the newly-devised technique of skip bombing, which proved so deadly in the Battle of the Bismarck Sea.

Behind the battle fronts, important trends were under way. At the Casablanca conference early in 1943 the percentage of Allied resources devoted to the Pacific and Asia was raised from a parsimonious 15% to a higher, although unspecified, figure.

American industrial might was giving muscle to the war effort. Although both Japan and the U.S. ended 1942 with few aircraft carriers, the U.S. initiated a large-scale carrier building program that produced the highly successful *Essex* class carriers, as well as numerous escort carriers to cover amphibious operations.

The results were of course not immediately evident and from a Philippine perspective the progress of the Allied forces in the Southwest Pacific seemed agonizingly slow. For a year and a half starting in mid-1942 we would hear of Allied victories but they took place two to three thousand miles away and gave no promise of early liberation.

THE PACE QUICKENS

But from late 1943 and particularly early 1944 the pace picked up. Nimitz's Central Pacific Forces took the Gilbert Islands, then the Japanese Marshall Islands. MacArthur leap-frogged to Hollandia in Dutch New Guinea in April and the following month was in Biak and then Numfoor Island off the northwestern tip of New Guinea, within flying distance of Mindanao.

The Philippines had by then become an important staging point for Japanese forces proceeding to the Southwest Pacific. They now assembled a considerable naval force at Tawi-Tawi that could counter threats from both New Guinea and the Marianas. They intended to attack MacArthur's latest advances, but the invasion of the Marianas was supervened, and they hurriedly sent their fleet to the northeast.

What followed was the Battle of the Philippine Sea, in which they lost three aircraft carriers and about 450 planes. It meant the destruction of their naval aviation, and after that their remaining carriers were toothless tigers with few planes and pilots. They had counted on the longer range of their planes and on the use of island airfields to shuttle their planes back and forth. The Americans, however, had learned of their basic plans from documents captured by the Cebu Guerrillas from a plane crash that killed Japanese fleet commander Admiral Koga. The island airfields were heavily bombed unknown to Japanese Admiral Ozawa, and his planes were met by a swarm of fighters and a line of warships with anti-aircraft guns. The battle became known as the Marianas Turkey Shoot.

LIBERATION CAMPAIGN BEGINS

Two months of fighting in the Marianas gave the Americans bases within B-29 range of the Japanese home islands. In MacArthur's sector the long battle for the liberation of the Philippines began with air raids on Davao in August. That was the same month in which Pres. Quezon died in the U.S., with Vice Pres. Osmeña now assuming the presidency. In mid-September the island of Morotai in the northern Moluccas was occupied, providing air bases within range of the Visayas.

That same month the aggressive Admiral Halsey commenced massive carrier raids starting with Mindanao and the Visayas on 9–14 September, then moving to Manila on the memorable dates of 21–22 September. Those were days of jubilation for Manilans who were again seeing American planes for the first time in over two and a half years. Great damage was done to airfields and shipping, and the sound of exploding vessels could be heard far into the night.

Halsey's famous Task Force 38 in the first 24 days of September destroyed over 1,000 Japanese planes and sank 150 ships of all types, for a loss of 72 aircraft.

Occupation Pres. Laurel, who had fended off Japanese demands to declare war on America when his "republic" was set up, now was compelled to take some action, and he came out with an ambiguously worded proclamation declaring the existence of a state of war with the U.S.

Halsey reported that he encountered only weak resistance, and the timetable for the liberation of the Philippines was accelerated. The planned landing on Mindanao was canceled, and the American invasion forces headed straight for Leyte, where they landed on

20 October, with MacArthur and Pres. Osmeña went ashore the first day to re-establish the Commonwealth government on Philippine territory. MacArthur, who had promised, "I shall return" when he left in 1942, now announced, "I have returned." Keeping this difficult promise raised his stature in Filipino eyes.

This set the stage for fierce land battles. Newly appointed over-all Japanese Commander Gen. Yamashita was ordered, against his better judgment, to send as many men as possible to Leyte, some of whom came from as far as Manchuria, and thousands perished on transport ships sunk by American carrier planes.

HISTORY'S LARGEST NAVAL BATTLE

This was also the setting for the largest naval battle in history, which was fought in Philippine waters. Four Japanese Naval forces converged on Leyte seeking to destroy the invasion forces. A southern force composed of two battleships, a cruiser and four destroyers under Adm. Nishimura went up Surigao Strait and was wiped out (except for one destroyer) by the U.S. 7th Fleet in the classical naval maneuver known as crossing the T, the last time in history that this would be accomplished. The Second Striking Force following 40 miles behind under Adm. Shima turned back on seeing the debacle, losing a cruiser in the move.

The main central force under Adm. Kurita sailed through the Sibuyan Sea, was attacked by both submarines and aircraft, and lost several cruisers and the super battleship *Musashi*, the largest in the world.

But the over-eager Halsey was lured away by the fourth Japanese force, a decoy fleet built around four virtually useless carriers. These plus a cruiser and two destroyers were sunk.

But Halsey had incautiously left San Bernardino Strait unguarded even by a picket vessel, and Kurita's diminished but still powerful main force—four battleships, six heavy and two light cruisers, and 11 destroyers—sailed through undisturbed in a feat of skillful night navigation and fell on some surprising escort carriers in the early morning. These sent up as many planes as they could, and also had their accompanying destroyers and destroyer escorts attack the battleships and heavy cruisers of Kurita's forces, making them break formation.

Kurita recalled his ships to reorganize his force but, although only 45 miles from his objective, did not renew the attack—evidently he thought he faced superior forces—and instead turned back, a controversial move that generated much argument later.

Many sailors from the sunken Japanese warships swam or were washed ashore. Some were taken to American ships on *bancas* by Filipinos. Others were killed by an irate population embittered by nearly three years of cruel oppression.

Toward the end of the battle new players made their first appearance, the Kamikaze suicide pilots. Based in Davao, Cebu, and Mabalacat, their first targets were the escort carriers. While most of them were shot down short of their objectives those who got through sank or damaged several of their targets. While the Kamikaze never stopped nor even delayed any military operation, they did cause damage and casualties. Their role in the Philippines was relatively limited and they were used to a much greater degree in the battle for Okinawa. Fear of the Kamikaze may have been one of the reasons for dropping the atom bomb.

The Battle of Leyte Gulf has been called a "shattering defeat" for the Japanese. They lost, in addition to the four carriers, three battleships, ten cruisers and nine destroyers. Many other ships were damaged, and for weeks after the battle American planes continued to hunt down and sink the survivors from the battle. The Americans lost only one light carrier, two escort carriers, two destroyers and one destroyer-escort.

The land fighting on Leyte continued into December with Japanese reinforcements who escaped air attacks landing at Ormoc and Palompon. The Japanese even tried sending in parachute troops, to little avail.

By mid-December the Americans had leaped across the Philippines to land on southern Mindoro in preparation for the invasion of Luzon.

FIGHTING RETURNS TO LUZON

All through the Leyte and Mindoro campaigns American carrier planes conducted weekly raids on targets in Luzon and especially Manila. Later they were joined by land-based planes. Civilian life became more difficult. Classes stopped, and some families were evacuated to the provinces. Prices of foodstuffs soared. By January 1945 people with bodies bloated by beriberi were dying beside garbage cans. Men were picked off the streets for forced labor on military defense projects, some never to return home. The *Kempeitai* grew more repressive, and most of those picked up in the waning days of the Occupation were never seen again.

On 24 December, it was announced that all wheeled vehicles, including bicycles and pushcarts, were subject to confiscation on sight. People had to walk to get around. Cars that had stood idle in garages since 1942 were suddenly visited and seized by Japanese intent on getting out of the city.

Japanese troops had numbered about 50,000 in mid-1943. Now the Luzon force alone numbered over 270,000 men, or triple the number of the USAFFE's Luzon force in 1941. Yamashita did not contest the landing at Lingayen Gulf on 9 January 1945 but divided his forces into three: the Shobu group of over 150,000 men in the Cordillera, the Kembu group of about 30,000 in the Zambales Mountains and the Shimbu group of about 50,000 in the mountains east of Manila. There were other units in Bicol and Batangas.

MacArthur's land commander, Gen. Walter Krueger of the 6th Army, proceeded carefully and methodically at a slower pace than Homma had followed in December 1941. Perhaps he wanted to guard his flanks against attacks from the mountain ranges bordering the northern part of the central plain of Luzon.

MANILA: LIBERATION AND DESTRUCTION

Yamashita had evacuated Manila for Baguio around Christmas, 1944 taking Laurel and several high officials with him. Some of these officials tried to get him to declare Manila an open city, as MacArthur had done in 1941, but he declined to do so formally, saying that this might bring in an American parachute landing from Mindoro. He said he would just quietly move his troops and let the Americans notice that they were gone.

But in the meantime about 12,000 Japanese Imperial marines from Cavite under Adm. Sanji Iwabuchi moved into Manila and started building defense works in the city. They joined around 4,000 army troops left by Yamashita supposedly to guard and destroy military supplies, but why it was taking them weeks to do this, when MacArthur had accomplished it in a few hours in 1941, calls into question the veracity of his supposed intention not to offer combat in the city.

The principal American unit driving toward Manila was the 37th Infantry Division. Toward the end of January, special operations were mounted. Possibly to avoid a repetition of the Puerto Princesa massacre of 139 American POWs on 14 December 1944, a raid was conducted, with considerable Filipino guerrilla assistance, on the Cabanatuan prison camp, where only 511 Allied (mostly American) POWs remained (the rest had died or been shipped off to Japan).

More significantly for combat operations, the 1st Cavalry Division was brought in from Leyte, and a motorized "Flying Column" of between 700 and 800 men was formed together with elements of the 44th Tank Battalion. They formed three groups or "Serials" and jumped off from Guimba, Nueva Ecija, just after midnight on 1 February.

The first Serial probably entered the city at 5 p.m. on Saturday, 3 February, and reached Malacañang Palace half an hour later. My uncle Jose who lived across the street said there was still daylight in the sky.

The second Serial came into the city shortly after and headed for the Santo Tomas Internment Camp. We were at after-dinner family rosary at our home in Balic-Balic about a mile away when around 7 p.m. we heard yelling from the direction of Santo Tomas, as well as seeing bright lights.We feared that the internees were being massacred, but when we checked with a relative living nearby, he said the Americans had arrived and the yelling was joyful cheering. There had been rumors that the internees were scheduled to be massacred on 5 February, but the rumors were unverified. Quite the contrary in fact, on 4 February the American prisoners and former Baguio internees in Old Bilibid Prison were left free by their guards, many of whom were Taiwanese who may have melted into Manila's Chinatown, whose Hokkien language they spoke, rather than proceeding to the combat area in the eastern hills.

The first two serials of the *Flying Column* had reached their objectives. The third serial which came later and was supposed to take the Legislative Building, however, ran into strong resistance at Far Eastern University and was prevented from crossing heavily defended Quezon Bridge.

This was dynamited, along with the other Pasig river bridges, the following day. Almost as soon as the presence of the Americans was known fires began in many parts of the city. It had been obvious for some time that the Japanese would not declare Manila an open city.

February 1945 should have been the most joyful month in Philippine history, bringing as it did our long-desired liberation. Instead, it turned into the most terrible and tragic month, at the end of which our capital was a scene of devastation overhung with the stench of death. In the most vicious crime in our history 100,000 innocent non-combatants had died. The military dead were almost all the 16,000 Japanese defenders and 1,000 Americans.

It was the only Allied capital in the Pacific to be destroyed, and the Japanese had left it almost uninhabitable, having destroyed its electric power, gas, telephone, and public transportation facilities. For a while, Manila was also without water, but with foresight, the American commanders achieved the early capture of the nearby water facilities, and some water service was restored after two weeks.

The Japanese military defense consisted simply of building up strong points—the electric power plant, Rizal Memorial Stadium, the University of the Philippines, the new Police Station and their last bastions: the Post Office, the Manila City Hall, the Legislative Building, the Finance and Agriculture Buildings and historic Intramuros.

ATROCITIES ON CIVILIANS

Manila north of the Pasig suffered less than the south side, but saw some death and destruction. The army troops (not marines) holding this part of the city dynamited buildings along the Escolta, committed some massacres and incendiarism in Tondo, and burned the commercial-residential portion of Santa Cruz just west of Quiapo church. Soldiers stationed themselves on the upper floors of the Great Eastern Hotel and shot at the people fleeing along the streets.

Santo Tomas was shelled from the south, killing about two dozen of the newly liberated internees as well as some Filipinos residing in the vicinity, including a distant relative of mine. Sampaloc Church and several adjacent commercial and residential blocks were destroyed by incendiary shells. There was also some long-distance shelling, apparently random and indiscriminate, from the Antipolo hills. One such shell landed about 100 yards from a neighbor's house where I was visiting at the time. Fortunately it fell in an open space.

The atrocities committed by the Japanese marines south of the Pasig river, mostly in Paco, Ermita, Malate, and Intramuros were appalling and ghastly. There were massacre sites too numerous to mention—De La Salle College, Pax Court, Concordia College, St. Paul's College, the German Club, the Price mansion, the Moreta house, the Philippine Red Cross, Intramuros of course, and other places.

Many of the atrocities committed had previously been seen in the Rape of Nanking in 1937—shooting, beheading, skewering babies on the points of bayonets, seizing young children by the legs and bashing their heads against walls, bayonetting pregnant women, and gouging out the fetuses, raping women and slicing them open from groin to the throat. At one massacre site, a dead Filipina lay with a bayonet through her genitals.

At the Bayview Hotel, the Japanese gathered the women of Ermita, then raped those they could. One young girl whom they had difficulty entering had her genitals enlarged by a pocket knife. The older women tried to protect the younger ones by placing themselves nearest the door and offering themselves to the Japanese. Some prostitutes among them, including some Russian women, played a heroic role in deflecting Japanese attention from the younger girls.

The Americans got to Intramuros on 17 February, but the Japanese had started burning the place as early as 7 February, when the Americans were just crossing the Pasig. What the Americans shelled in their final assault was the burned-out hulk of the storied city.

When the battle concluded on 3 March 1945, so many homes had been burned that one could see clear through from Taft Avenue to Manila Bay. For months thereafter the stench of death hting over the ruined metropolis.

RESPONSIBILITY FOR MANILA'S DESTRUCTION

When one asks who destroyed Manila and killed its inhabitants, it is easy to say that both contending forces had a part. MacArthur had forbidden the use of air power, but could not prevent the ground commanders from calling in artillery fire, which was some times excessive and indiscriminate. One such tragic case was the shelling of Remedios Hospital, clearly marked by a large red cross on its roof and under observation by American artillery spotter planes. But there can be no moral equivalence between them. It was the Japanese who chose to make Manila a battleground, and even worse, a killing ground. And it is a mystery what possible military objective was accomplished by the slaughter of non-combatants, the destruction of historic structures, and the rape of innocent women.

Who gave the order for Manila's holocaust? Field orders have been found detailing how civilians were to be killed with the least expenditure of ammunition. Did the orders originate from Adm. Sanji Iwabuchi, the Butcher of Manila? In the divided Japanese command system, although he was operationally under Yamashita, he followed orders from his naval superiors like Southwest Asia Fleet Commander Vice-Admiral Denshichi Okochi. It was Okochi who ordered the building of defenses in Manila in the second half of December 1944 before going to Baguio with Yamashita, who must have known what was going on. The orders may even have come from as high as Tokyo, but they may never be found because the Japanese had two weeks between their surrender and the start of the American occupation to destroy incriminating documents.

Yamashita himself professed to know nothing about the sack of Manila, although Domei news dispatches received at his headquarters in Baguio carried news about it. He claimed he could no longer communicate with units in the field, an incredible claim since, if the Filipino guerrillas, with their rudimentary radio sets, could communicate with Australia, why could he not contact Manila and southern Luzon from Baguio?

The Rape of Manila was followed by similar atrocities in southern Luzon—Batangas, Laguna, and Tayabas. Herminio "Miniong" Ordonez writes that "The Japanese soldiers turned very vicious and barbaric," burning San Pablo, Santa Cruz, Lucban and other big towns, killing even women and children and tossing babies in the air and catching them with their bayonets (Ordonez, *Gut Feel*, 52).

Perhaps 50,000 civilians or more perished, and the killers were not marines but army troops under Col. Masatoshi Fujishige. In their area they suffered the humiliation of having about 2,000 meters at Los Baños liberated by a mixed force, with the Filipino guerrillas doing most of the fighting. This led to reprisals against civilians.

LIBERATION OF OTHER ISLANDS

MacArthur was in a hurry to liberate the rest of the Philippines, despite the indifference of the Joint Chiefs of Staff and less than a month after the Luzon campaign started he put his plans into motion, even if it meant diverting forces from Luzon and delaying its reconquest. He did not want to leave Filipino civilians in the bypassed islands at the mercy of the increasingly desperate and brutal Japanese. He also wanted to establish air bases in Palawan, 150 miles farther west than Clark or Mindoro, in order to interdict Japanese communications in the China Sea, and other bases on Zamboanga and Sulu to support the planned reconquest of Borneo and the East Indies.

On some islands there was only brief fighting. On Panay the guerrillas were in almost total control, and greeted the American landing in parade formation. The Japanese burned Iloilo City before retreating, but this did not stop the laughing, cheering, and flower-throwing citizens crazy with joy. Bohol had only a small garrison and was taken easily without serious damage. But Cebu City was destroyed almost as thoroughly as Manila.

The sequence of landings in the southern areas was the following:

19–20 Feb	NW Samar, Dalupiri, Capul, Biri
28 Feb	Puerto Princesa, Palawan
3 March	Burias and Ticao
10 March	Zamboanga
16 March	Panay
18 March	Cebu
26 March	Negros

29 March	Legaspi
1 April	Tawi-Tawi
2 April	Masbate
9 April	Jolo, Busuanga
11 April	Bohol
17 April	Cotabato
3 May	Davao Gulf
10 May	Macajalar Bay (N. Mindanao)

On most islands the pattern of operations was for the Americans to subdue organized Japanese resistance and mostly withdraw, leaving the mopping-up to the Filipino guerrillas. On Panay, for example, it was the Filipino guerrillas who virtually wiped out the 300-man Japanese garrison in San Jose de Buenavista, capital of Antique province.

Only on Luzon, Mindanao, Negros, and perhaps Cebu did Japanese military strength require the prolonged presence of American combat units. Of the total Japanese troops strength of 381,550 in the Philippines (about four times the 1941 USAFFE numbers) 275,685 or 72% were on Luzon, 64,750 or 17% on Mindanao, 14,900 or 3.9% on Negros and 14,500 or 3.8% on Cebu— all in all 97% of total Japanese troops in the country. (R.R. Smith, *Triumph in the Philippines*, 604).

FILIPINO GUERRILLA VICTORIES

On Luzon the fighting continued after the destruction of Manila. A Mexican fighter squadron lent its support, the only deployment of Mexican armed forces outside Mexico's borders, in consideration of its former historical ties with the Philippines.

The Filipino guerrillas scored two notable victories. One was the taking of Ipo Dam on 17 May, which assured an ample water supply for Manila, which was growing into a staging area for American military operations, including preparations for the invasion of Japan.

The other was the capture of Bessang Pass on the western slopes of the Cordillera Central on 14 June. This was important because the Shobu Group's defense triangle was anchored on Baguio, Bambang, and Bontoc. With Baguio having fallen Bessang Pass opened the way to Bontoc, which was occupied on 10 July.

The Shobu Group was compressed into the Kiangan pocket after Filipino guerrillas and American forces linked up on 21 July five miles north of Banaue. When Japan surrendered on 15 August, the Filipino guerrillas were only five miles from Yamashita's headquarters.

In the final phase of the Luzon campaign, which involved the Cagayan Valley all the churches, except those in the northwest corner, were bombed by American planes, resulting in a great cultural loss. This stood in marked contrast to the care taken by the Americans to avoid bombing the Japanese cultural center of Kyoto. Fortunately the Cagayan structures were built solidly enough for the walls at least to remain standing.

By the time Japan surrendered, the Kembu and Shimbu groups had lost to death over 90% of their number. The Shobu group had lost 63%. On Luzon as a whole Japanese killed were 75% of the total; in the southern islands, the percentage was just under 50%.

Yamashita supposedly wanted to tie up as many American troops and cause enough casualties to delay the expected invasion of the home islands. His success is in some doubt. There were increasing numbers of Filipino guerrillas available to relieve American troops for other duties.

Besides, even as the fighting was going on, the Philippines was being built up as a staging area for the projected invasion.

In 1942 the USAFFE had denied the Japanese the use of Manila Bay and the Port of Manila for over four months.

In 1945 American ships, after the quick conquest of Corregidor by combined paratroops and amphibious forces, entered Manila Bay less than six weeks after the land forces reached Manila.

MANILA AFTER THE BATTLE

How had Manila changed since the last days of the Japanese Occupation? As already seen more than half the city was destroyed and 100,000 of its inhabitants were killed. Public utilities were almost non-existent, except for water service which was restored fairly quickly. The bridges over the Pasig had been demolished.

The cultural devastation was appalling. The good theatre stages had been destroyed, as well as all, except two, of the first-run movie houses. Centuries-old churches were in ruins, as were stately mansions. Professor Santiago Pilar estimates that a very large part of our artistic heritage was lost. When the Manila Symphony emerged from its non-collaborationist hibernation the first postliberation concert it gave took place in the roofless ruins of Santa Cruz Church, on 9 May 1945, with Beethoven's monumental Eroica symphony to honor the Allied war dead. In human terms, the country's leading violinist, Ernesto Vallejo, was massacred in his home province in Batangas together with his family. Composer Juan S. Hernandez was killed by a Japanese grenade together with his family during the battle for Manila. The manuscript for Francisco Santiago's symphony was burned, and it exists only in a rendition from memory by Antonino Buenaventura.

Everyday life changed drastically. The transportation shortages gave way to an abundance of jeeps, weapons carriers and six-by-sixes. Canned goods became plentiful. There were no more bodies bloated with beriberi beside garbage cans.

Teams of American health workers went from house to house pouring disinfectants into pools of stagnant water and even large jars *(tapayan)* which might be breeding places for mosquitoes, while overhead planes made frequent runs spraying DDT. People were free to talk again without furtively looking over their shoulders for informers.

There were also little mundane details. Clocks were back on Manila Standard time, no longer an hour ahead on Greater East Asia Standard Time. And starting at the beginning of June, 1945 traffic flowed on the right, American style, rather than on the left as in pre-war Days, British and Japanese style. The police abandoned their pre-war. London Bobby-style helmets and adopted American military caps.

ECONOMIC STATE

Economically, the picture was laced with irony. Japan had, sincerely or not, professed to fight the war against western colonialism. Yet it left the economy in such devastation, dysfunctional in fact, and the Philippine infrastructure in such ruin that it produced the opposite effect. Philippine progress toward independence before the war envisioned a process of lessening its overdependence on the American economy. Instead, after the war, it found itself more dependent than ever on America. Prof. Gerardo Sicat of the U.P. Economics Department estimates that post-war output was only 30% of the 1940 level.

Food production, insufficient even in pre-war days for the needs of the population, was sharply lower after the fighting. Export crops fared even worse. The principal export crop, sugar, suffered a reduction in hectarage of nearly 90%. Coconuts and abaca did not decrease as much but there was no replanting, and neglect allowed weeds and jungle growth to encroach on these areas. Livestock was reduced by 63%. Carabaos, the main draft animals, were down by 54%. Mining production stopped completely.

These were badly damaged economic bases on which to build political independence.

LOOKING FORWARD

But with the restoration of freedom, there was optimism. Marcial P. Lichauco wrote (*Dear Mother Putnam*, 219–220): "To our country as a whole this war may prove to be a blessing in diguise... We were beginning to be afraid of independence and the sacrifice it would require from all of us... Now the situation is different. Today the whole world knows us and every man and woman living in the Islands is proud to be a Filipino... We may stumble and we may fall, but we shall rise again with courage and renewed hope. And we will win in the end for we are no longer afraid."

Ordeal of Baguio During World War II

Oscar M. Lopez

Mr. Ambeth Ocampo, National Historical Institute chairman, Mr. Benito Legarda, NHI director, officers and members of the National Historical Institute, ladies and gentlemen, good afternoon. Never did I envision that I would be giving a talk about Baguio during the war. Nevertheless, I am now in front of you, giving this talk. If ever there must be someone to blame for this state of affairs, I submit that the fault lies squarely on Mrs. Maribel Ongpin, who is here with us this afternoon, widow of the late Jimmy Ongpin. She told Beniting Legarda about my 6-hour trek from Irisan to Asin last April in my attempt to relive in a small way my three-day trek to freedom during the ending days of the war in Baguio 60 years ago. One thing led to another, and Beniting called me up, requesting me to give this 30-minute talk about the ordeal of Baguio. Besides, how can you refuse two respected and dear friends! Thus, if

I fumble and do not meet your expectations, you know whom to blame. Nevertheless, if only to exonerate Mrs. Ongpin, we interviewed her, and she gave an excellent recollection of Baguio during the war, particularly the carpet bombing and subsequent trek down the mountains.

As to my methodology, there are two things I want to say: First, I am using as many as possible first person accounts or references to such. I start with myself. I will give my recollections of my experiences about Baguio during the war. Though not a native of Baguio, I was in Baguio at the start of the war. I was 11 years old then; and I was also there during the last two and half years of the war up to April 1945. By that time, I was 15 years old, admittedly still young in age but old enough to know what was going on in the world. Believe me, when you have been subjected to almost daily bombing for a period of several months, you will always remember that phase of your life no matter how young you were at the time or how long ago the bombings took place. My staff has also interviewed persons who were in Baguio during the war; the interviewees were in both Baguio and Manila. Finally, I interspersed personal reminiscences with authoritative accounts from books and magazine articles about the war. Second, regarding scope, I divided my talk into periods, namely, the start of the war, the years of Japanese occupation, and the bombing and liberation of Baguio by the Americans and trek to freedom from Baguio to Tubao, La Union. At the end I will discuss the issue of the carpet bombing of Baguio by the Americans and why they did it.

The key persons interviewed were:

1. Mrs. Maribel Ongpin—columnist, staunch social change advocate, and civic leader;

2. Mrs. Ruby Roxas—daughter of Gen./Pres. Manuel Roxas;

3. Mrs. Virginia De Guia—former mayor of Baguio City;

4. Mrs. Cecile Carino-Afable—editor of the *Baguio Midland Courier*;

5. Judge Fernando Cabato (retired); and

6. Mr. John Silva, Senior Consultant, National Museum.

7. Mr. Albert Montilla, an avid photo collector who provided most of WWII photos and of Baguio, shown here this afternoon.

8. Finally, helping me put all the materials together are Cesar Gomez, head of the Communications Dept, of FPHC, assisted by Nicole Carlos; Raul Rodrigo, author of *Phoenix the Saga of the Lopez Family* and other books on Lopez businesses; my executive assistant, Margot Fragante; and, finally, the Staff of the Lopez Museum.

So much for the introduction to my speech, let me now start the storytelling.

BAGUIO BEFORE THE WAR

My extended stay in Baguio started in June 1939. My elder brother, Eugenio, Junior or Geny, and I started school in the Maryknoll Convent School, a coed grade school run by American Maryknoll nuns. The great majority of the students in that school were American children of expats working in the mines around Baguio. Filipinos like me represented only about 20–30% of the students in Maryknoll. I would like to state that at this period of my life I learned how to play good basketball in Maryknoll from Fr. James Reuter, S.J., who was a young scholastic at that time. We lived on Paterno Street in an area known as South Drive, which only a few kilometers from both Baguio Country Club and Camp John Hay.

Due to lovely weather and his certainty of Baguio land prices quickly appreciating in value, my father invested heavily in local real estate. He built the Lopez Building, which sprawled over an entire block on Session Road, during the Nineteen Thirties. By school year 1940–41, my uncle, Vicente Arenas sent his second son Mariano to live and study alongside us in Maryknoll.

I think it is more poignant to end this portion of Baguio before the war by simply projecting pictures of Baguio before the war. The nostalgia brought about by the pictures should add drama to the following sections.

THE START OF THE WAR IN BAGUIO

It was 8 December 1941, the Feast of the Immaculate Conception, so we all went to Mass at the Baguio Cathedral at 7:00 a.m. Earlier that morning at 5:00 a.m., we got a call from our Tita Aurora Recto, wife of Don Claro Recto, and godmother of my sister Presy, telling us that her husband received reports that Pearl Harbor was bombed by Japanese planes. Shortly after 8:00 a.m. I was practicing on the violin at home when we, Geny, Mariano, and I, heard the roar of many aircraft. We all ran out of the house. We saw this huge formation, of about 20 twin-engine bomber planes heading straight for Camp John Hay. We initially thought they were American planes, practicing flying. So we waved at them, then we saw little black things, looking like eggs, falling from the planes. Only after we heard the explosions did we realize that we saw some of the very first Japanese bombs to hit Philippine soil right in Camp John Hay.

When my father, who was then in Iloilo, was informed, he instructed us to go to Manila immediately, where we were to wait for word from him where he would send his INAEC commercial plane to pick us up. We all hurriedly packed for the dash down Kennon Road. What were my thoughts then? Like kids, initially, we felt happy because there were "no more classes!" To us then, war sounded like a big exciting adventure. I remember that our driver drove down Kennon Rod at a terrific speed the afternoon of the same day. When we crossed Tarlac to Pampanga, we saw black smoke rising high into the sky; the Japanese bombed Clark and Iba airfields in a surprise and devastating air raid that same day of 8 December. After staying in Manila for a few days, where we also experienced the first bombing in Manila, we proceeded to Batangas, where we caught the INAEC Sikorsky amphibian plane for Iloilo.

We stayed in Iloilo for a few months. During that time, we also experienced the first Japanese bombing in Iloilo City which destroyed all of my father's commercial planes belonging to the Iloilo-Negros Air Express Co. or

INAEC. At the same time, my father had two important visitors in Iloilo. The first was President Quezon, a close friend to my father, who had just escaped by submarine from Corregidor on 22 February 1942, and was on his way to Australia. As kids we were thrilled to see our President, but he looked so old and weak that he had to be carried in a chair up the stairs to the farm house in Dingle where we had evacuated. That was to be the last meeting between the two old friends. On 9 April, Lt. Col. Carlos P. Romulo, another close friend of my father, arrived by plane from Bataan. It was only upon his arrival that Romulo heard on the radio that Bataan had surrendered. He was in tears when he talked about Bataan and Corregidor. He said he too was on his way to Australia.

When the Japanese landed in Iloilo, my father brought his family first to the mountains in Dingle, then after a few months we crossed over to Negros Occidental where we stayed for a few more months at the Lopez Sugar Central, trying to decide where we wanted to spend the rest of the war years. My father finally decided on Baguio where he had his Lopez building right on Session Road and he liked the people and the weather there. Before the end of 1942, we were all in Baguio.

BAGUIO UNDER THE JAPANESE OCCUPATION

The Japanese landed in Lingayen on 22 December 1941 and were quickly up in Baguio by 27 December. There was no opposition encountered at all as the Japanese came up the Naguilian Road to Baguio. A delegation composed of Mayor Valderrosa, the American vice-mayor, Mr. Hayakawa (president of the Japanese Association), and Chief of Police Keith met the Japanese at Km. 4 on Naguilian Road and implored the Japanese to spare the city. To avoid further loss of life and property, Baguio was declared an open city. Three trucks full of Japanese soldiers entered the city before lunch and first set up headquarters at the Japanese School.

The years under the Japanese Occupation—I think it can be said that the years from 1942 till the latter part of 1944 were relatively peaceful years of Japanese occupation.

During the early part of our stay in Baguio, we encountered a gentlemanly and civilized Japanese military commander, a certain General Nagasaki. He had good relations with the Filipinos. He enjoyed walking along Session Road in civilian clothes without bodyguards. In his book *A Diary of the Japanese Occupation*, Fr. Juan Labrador, O.P., former rector of Letran and U.S.T. mentioned meeting General Nagasaki at a banquet given by the religious branch of the Japanese army at Pines Hotel on 8 May 1942. He said "I have never seen a Japanese so courteous, jolly and witty...This man has traveled and lived in Europe where two of his daughters were converted to Catholicism." Unfortunately, he was transferred to Davao before the end of 1942 and was replaced by a hardliner militarist. Before he left however, he gave our family a present, a beautiful Cocker Spaniel dog which was owned and abandoned by the American owner of the house he was occupying in Baguio. Let me just add this postscript to the General Nagasaki story.

After the war was over, in the course of one of his business trip to Tokyo, my father made it a point to look for General Nagasaki. With the help of his Japanese businessmen friends, he found him in the Jesuit-run Sophia University. He was apparently working as handyman in that school. When my father and I addressed him as General, he shook his head and said "Now, no more general. Now just plain civilian." He added that, like his daughters, he was now a Catholic.

Of course, Japanese atrocities were also experienced in Baguio because of the Japanese military police or *Kempeitai* who were always looking for suspected guerrillas. The *Kempeitai* established its headquarters in the International Harvester building and an adjoining cold storage area in July 1942. Then the *Kempeitai* Headquarters was generally known as the "cooler" or "freezer," where many Filipinos were imprisoned and tortured. I still remember the only public execution held in Baguio. It must have been toward the end of 1942 or early 1943. Four Igorots and one Ilocano were summarily executed without trial at the market plaza and many people were taken from Session Road and other streets of Baguio to witness the spectacle. I remember Geny and I wanted to watch but my father refused to allow us to go. We learned later that two were shot and the other three were beheaded with samurai swords.

But in general, the period 1942 to 1944 was considered a "lay-low" period by the guerrillas of northern Luzon on order by the Southwest Pacific Area Command (SWPA) under General MacArthur.

In a message sent by MacArthur to USAFIP-NL (for Northern Luzon) on March 1943, he asked the guerrilla organization headed by Colonel Russell Volckmann to limit hostilities and contact with the enemy to the minimum. USAFIP-NL would instead concentrate on perfecting organization and on developing an intelligence network, until ammunitions and supplies could be sent. The arms did not start coming in until November and December of 1944 shortly before the American landing in Lingayen.

Let me quote Maribel Ongpin who gives a good description of how the Japanese made their presence felt in Baguio in other ways: She says, "one was by confiscating cars and vehicles of private citizens and businesses. People tried to negotiate to keep their cars and vehicles but were rarely successful. My father's car, my aunt's car, and, many friends cars were all confiscated. Next, the Japanese expropriated buildings and houses for their purposes. One wing of the Vallejo Hotel which was owned by my grandfather was taken for some kind of communications activity. A huge antenna was placed on the roof, and some officers held office there. Third, the Japanese drafted men for forced labor in roads and bridges near Baguio."

War was a time of shortages. Concerning the economy, basic items were scarce.

Money was also a problem with inflation causing items to cost astronomical sums in Japanese-issued currency. But there was one good side to wartime inflation. Debt incurred in hard currency before the War could be paid in inflated currency during the Occupation and the courts accepted this principle. Since my father refused to deal in buy and sell operations, especially with the Japanese during this time, he was content to sell some of his properties to settle debt and live peacefully with everyone. Anyway, he had already lost all his businesses in Iloilo. All the Iloilo-Negros Air Express or INAEC planes were destroyed by the Japanese, all the buses of Panay Autobus were commandeered by the Philippine Army, and his newspapers, *Iloilo Times* and *El Tiempo*, stopped publication when he left Iloilo and the Japanese took over. The name of the game at that time was the survival of the family and you chose your residence in a town, in a barrio, or up in the mountains, depending on where you thought you could get maximum safety. Everything else was secondary to this objective. And there would be ample time to think about starting new businesses after the war.

Schooling resumed. Elders whiled away the time by socializing with other residents every afternoon at Session Road. Maribel's relative remembered participating in tea sessions at the Tropicana Cafe in the Lopez Building, which was followed by blackjack card games with bets. Some played golf in the mornings, while others walked Burnham Park where the young ones skated.

The Japanese did not have a heavy presence in Baguio during the early part of the War. It was only from October 1944 onwards that the bulk of the 150,000 troops designated to defend North Luzon and Baguio started on taking their positions on Kennon and Naguilian Roads and other strategic locations in Northern Luzon.

As to my family, as I said, we were all back in Baguio by the end of 1942. We stayed in a bungalow at the back of the Lopez Building on Session Road for the next two years. Geny and I continued our schooling first at St. Louis School, a school run by Belgian nuns just behind the Lopez Bldg. For a while we even had lessons in Nipongo. But when St. Louis closed during the start of the bombings, my father, who was always concerned that we continue our studies, had all of us, Geny, our cousin Benito Lopez, Ramon and Mariano Arenas, and I walked several kilometers three times a week to the La Salle Retreat House, across Burnham Park, where Brother Alphonse taught us chemistry and Brother Felix taught typing. This was supplemented by additional walks in the afternoon to the St. Scholastica's Convent where we took up English literature and other subjects.

Many people also went up to Baguio, including other prominent families. My father encountered tycoons from Iloilo and Manila—Nicolas Lizares, Placido Mapa, Senen Gabaldon, Oscar Ledesma, Salvador Araneta, and the entire Cacho clan and Cojuangco clan. Due to the war, people had so much time on their hands.

My father established ties with the guerrillas in the surrounding mountains through friends or relations in the City. One such friend was Esperanza Enriquez, wife of Capt. Manolo Enriquez, a PMA graduate who became a guerrilla leader but was eventually caught by the Japanese and executed in Fort Santiago. Parties would often be organized in the Tropicana Cafe in the Lopez building to raise money for food and medicine for the guerrillas. At the same time, my father also established contacts with the Japanese, thereby enabling him to better help friends but more importantly to help ensure the survival of his family. As Mrs. Enriquez wrote in her book, *A War Widow's Experience*:

> The civilian most respected by Japanese in the city was Don Eugenio Lopez, an Iloilo businessman with properties in Baguio. President Manuel Roxas and Don Claro Recto evacuated to Baguio and often attended social gatherings at Don Eugenio's house. On the many occasions when I attended his functions, I would see Chief of Military Police Capt. Harada, who enjoyed going to the parties of this bon vivant. Once during a New Year's celebration, he came with several Japanese officers and stayed on until the wee hours of the morning.

My father had a secret weapon for these parties. Since imported whiskey was very scarce, my father would pour locally distilled alcohol into White Label bottles and somehow the Japanese never complained about the taste and they got just as drunk on local as on imported whiskey.

Despite this relationship, my father was still picked up by the dreaded military police *Kempeitai* for questioning regarding a shortwave band radio found in the house of one of his friends where my father and his friends would meet every afternoon to listen to the news from newscaster William Winters thru radio station KGEI in San Francisco. Though the radio was confiscated, fortunately neither he nor his friends were punished, although the ultimate penalty for having or listening to shortwave radio was death. This is probably one instance where the good social relationship with the Japanese military paid off.

As the Americans started bombing Manila in September 1944, in preparation for the Leyte and Luzon landings, as the food situation in that city worsened, more prominent families moved to Baguio, such as the Tuasons, the Ferias, and the Guevarras. My father's in-laws, the whole Moreno clan and the Arenas family, also moved up in September 1944. Owning or having access to houses and apartments in Baguio, these families hoped to escape the envisioned heavy fighting in Manila for the supposedly peaceful, more serene and cooler heights of Baguio.

But there were mounting pressures on Baguio toward the latter part of 1944 onwards, pressure eventually led to the tragedy of the carpet bombing of Baguio and almost destruction of the city in the first four months of 1945.

First, as I have already said, Manila began to be bombed by American planes starting 21 September 1944. Then came the invasion of Leyte on 20 October 1944. The third was the arrival of General Yamashita from Manchuria in early October to take charge of the overall defense of the Philippines. Yamashita decided he could not defend Manila and Central Luzon because of its open flatlands. He also deliberately avoided the Bataan peninsula because he considered that cul-de-sac as a death trap. Instead, he organized his forces into three mountainous strongholds that could be overrun only at the cost of many lives and much time. The first, called the Kembu group, was located in the Zambales Mountain range on the western side of Central Luzon overlooking Clark Field with 30,000 men. The second was the Shimbu group that would concentrate on the mountains east and northeast of Manila with 80,000 troops, including 20,000 naval troops under Admiral Sanji Iwabuchi in Manila. The third known as the Shobu group was stationed in the various mountains east and northeast of Lingayen Gulf as well as the fertile Cagayan Valley. The Shobu group was directly responsible to

Yamashita and would have the largest contingent of 150,000 troops with headquarters in Baguio City itself. Further pressure was applied on Baguio when Gen. Yamashita required the Laurel government to transfer to Baguio by the end of December 1944. By then, Baguio had become the actual political and military center of the Philippines, not Manila anymore.

Just as the 8 December 1941 bombing of Baguio ushered in the war and Japanese invasion of the Philippines on 20 December 1941, so the first American bombing of Baguio on 6 January 1945 ushered in the American invasion of Luzon on 9 January, when one of the greatest armadas of all times ever assembled with 818 ships appeared in Lingayen Gulf. On 15–16 January, American planes came back and bombed City Hall and other parts of the town. Up to this point, most civilians still felt unconcerned about the bombing because it was done selectively and affected only government and public areas like the market place, and there were few casualties as yet.

But by February and March, bigger twin and four engine bombers joined the raids on Baguio, which meant the Americans had intentions of destroying the entire city.

By this time the civilians only had three choices:

1. Build good air raid shelters near their homes that could withstand heavy bombing.

2. Seek shelter in strong concrete structures like churches, schools, hospitals, convents, and office buildings.

3. Leave the city for safer outlying areas.

Those with access to enough manpower and time took the first option. Many more sought shelter in public buildings and the Baguio Cathedral became the favorite place for many. The third alternative was reserved as a last resort.

Maribel Ongpin has a good description of this period of the bombing: "When this period started the terrified populace left their homes, even their air-raid shelters near their homes and flocked to the Baguio Cathedral and Notre Dame Hospital. The Baguio Cathedral became crowded with refugees; some sort of order was installed thru the use of pews to demarcate spaces for families. Only women and children were allowed to be in the Cathedral except in air raids when the men could seek shelter. Still, it was so crowded that some men like my father and his friends decided to dig their air raid shelter in front, outside the Cathedral with a little makeshift hut on top of where they could while away their time in between raids. Life in Baguio revolved around the daily bombing raids."

Then came the air raid of February 16, when a single dive bomber dropped a bomb right in front of the big concrete cross, situated a few meters from the front of the Cathedral. Many civilians who built their shacks in this area including Maribel's father and his friends, were blown to bits by this one bomb. This is how Maribel described that bombing:

> When the bomb fell it brought on a louder, more deafening sound than usual, causing the stained glass windows to shatter. By intuition, my mother immediately knew that my father had died with that bomb...when the raid ended we saw his shack and all the other structures around it gone, and body parts all over the place.

> These events repeated themselves days and weeks afterward with people killed by shrapnel or direct hits. My cousin says there were so many casualties that a big hole was made on the Cathedral grounds to bury them and he helped bury at least 50 people in the course of our stay in the Cathedral.

It was after the 16 February bombing that many people began to review their options. The last raid was so deliberately done by a single dive bomber that there was no mistaking its message. The American planes were no longer looked upon as harbingers of deliverance and freedom but as instruments of cold-blooded, and indiscriminate death from the sky. For weeks, a small observation plane would drop leaflets saying civilians should stay away from military targets and apologized for the inconvenience or harm if civilians were near their targets.

It was implying that the entire city of Baguio was the target. What the Americans failed to realize was that shortly after the U.S. landing in Lingayen, while Baguio was technically still known as General Yamashita's Headquarters, Yamashita had moved his real defensive HQ some 80 kilometers north to a rugged mountainous area called Kiangan, considered by the U.S. Army official report as "one of the world's most ideal piece of defensive terrain—miles high mountains, rugged gorges, narrow valley, precipitous slopes..."

Given all the three options I listed above, my father who was responsible for the safety of more than 50 people in the extended family living in the Lopez Building, decided to look for a safer haven outside Baguio. One morning after 16 February, some male members of the group including myself accompanied my father on a hike down Naguilian Road. Some seven kilometers down was a *sitio* called Irisan. He met and befriended an Ibaloi native, named Sotero who was willing to accommodate the entire family on his land. For the next few weeks, all the men pitched in to dig several air raid shelters to accommodate everyone of the 50 in the family. We lived and slept in those air raid shelters for more than one month.

It was timely that we left Baguio City by the end of February, because between 4 and 10 March, according to official reports, the 5th Air Force planes on 910 sorties unloaded 933 tons of bombs and 1185 gallons of napalm in and around Baguio. The city shuddered under raid after raid.

Then on 15–17 March, Baguio would be subjected to its worst carpet bombing. One of those who documented this attack with official records from the army and air force was James J. Halsema son of E. J. Halsema who helped build Baguio and became its mayor for 17 years from 1920 to 1937, but who also died in Baguio that day of 15 March together with four other Americans in Notre Dame Hospital. This is what James Halsema said:

As the B-24s came in a mile (1,620 m.) above the city, they went into single file. Two squadrons discharged their loads from south to north, the two others from southwest to northeast. After bombing, each squadron broke left to return to base. The B-25s covered the target abreast. Altogether 170 planes—47 P-38s from Clark Field, 77 Fifth Air Force B-24s and B-25s from Mindoro and Mangaldan and 46 P-38s of the Thirteenth Air Force from Leyte came over Baguio that day to release their loads in boxes only 200 feet (61 meters) square patterns so dense and devastating that they were termed "carpet bombing." Many of the bombs were thousand pounders (455 kgs.). Their target was "troop concentrations—Baguio area." They were given the rote order: "Do not bomb unless the target is positively identified." An official report recorded routinely that in support of "ground troops attacking around Baguio...bomb hits were scored on staff quarters, barracks, a radio station, and many buildings in the government center. By nightfall the town appeared untenable." Even in the afternoon "smoke over the city precluded further assessment of the damage." Two days later pilots were still having difficulty seeing buildings through the black pall. "It was the end of downtown Baguio and of the man (his father) who had done so much to build it" lamented Jim Halsema.

I remember that morning and afternoon of 15 March, from our air-raid shelter in Irisan, we could see all the planes as they came to carpet bomb the city. We were thankful we left when we did because had we stayed many of us would have died in that bombing because the Lopez Building suffered many direct hits. That evening, hundreds of civilians were coming out of the city to Barrio Irisan or Long-Long, or some other places; some were wounded, some had lost loved ones, but they were all in a daze, not knowing where to go.

But our ordeal was not yet over. In fact, in between the two carpet bombings of Baguio, the Lopez family in Irisan encountered our own tragedy, because on 11 March, our uncle Nicholas Lizares was hit and killed by a long range artillery shell. His son Joseling was with him and he also suffered shrapnel wounds. But he survived. By the end of March, we became very impatient for the Americans to get to Baguio, so my father decided for the whole family to trek down to La Union. Many had already preceded us. By 30 March the first trickle of what was to be 7,000 refugees reached Manila. Among the first were Guillermo Guevarra and his family, Mr. Benjamin Jalandoni and family, Manny Locsin, Mr. and Mrs. Justo Arrastia and family. Major and Mrs. Conrado de Castro and children.

In our case, we left Irisan on 7 April 1945 at 4:30 am. When the sun rose, we could see hundreds of other refugees on the mountainsides, also hiking to the coast. We climbed so many mountains I could not keep count of them anymore. But every night we ended up on top of one of them; usually there was a shack where the women and children could lay down and sleep. All the men and boys had to sleep outside. My brother Manolo was only two years old. On the second day, he could no longer walk so Geny and I took turns carrying him on our backs. I remember also we encountered an old woman lying beside the trail in a crude lean-to with a little food beside her. She had been with a group but her legs had given out and her companions abandoned her on the trail. Many other groups, especially before us, also passed this old woman. But those who passed three or four days after us say that by then she was already dead. She pleaded to take her with us, but we had no one to spare to carry her. We all had our hands full to make sure the smaller children in our group could complete the journey. When we started the trek we carried so many things, extra clothes, towels, food, canteen, flashlight, knife, etc., but as you progressed up and down the mountains, you started shedding these things because, toward the latter part of the trek, you had barely enough strength to carry yourself. We also met some Japanese stragglers along the way, but all they wanted was food. On the late morning of the

3rd day, we were already on flat land with a river in the distance, and beside the river were many soldiers who at first looked like Japanese soldiers. When we got closer we realized they were Americans, and we all ran to them and shook their hands, some of us hugged them. We had just passed through the gates of hell and we were free at last. It no longer mattered that part of the hell that we went through was due to the American bombing. It no longer mattered that the Baguio we left behind was dead. But what was important was that we came out of that holocaust, that ordeal, alive, and I felt one day, Baguio would rise again, as indeed it has.

Just to round out our story, as we were coming down on 7 April the American troops of the 37th Infantry Division were fighting their way up Naguilian Road. They started on 7 April and by 26 April, they were in Baguio with the help of the USAFIP-NL contingents, the 66th Battalion made up of Baguio guerrillas like Bado Dangwa and Dennis Molintas. Incidentally, one of the last big battles fought between the Fil-American forces and the Japanese in the Naguilian Road was in Irisan and we would have been caught in the crossfire if we had delayed our trip down to Tubao any longer.

In the 22 May 2000 issue of the *Philippine Graphic*, the late Nick Joaquin wrote what seemed like a fitting epitaph for the old Baguio, entitled "When Baguio was killed." In part, the article said:

> The first American air raid in January 1945 had been rapturously hailed by Baguio, which had survived the years of the Japanese occupation in quite a good condition. What the evacuees returned to in May 1945 was a desolation of rot and ruin; a blackened highland that was once fragrant greenwood. The post liberation Baguio was charred hillside bereft of green or brown.

Nick Joaquin ends the story with this question, "Why did the Americans have to kill Baguio?" He did not answer this question, but we will try to do so now.

1. First of all, because Baguio was officially the headquarters of General Yamashita and as such, Baguio was a legitimate target for American aircraft. What also made Baguio very attractive as a target was because it was the second biggest supply depot of the Japanese army in Northern Luzon. Furthermore, every route to Baguio was held by crack troops of Yamashita, and for more than a month, every attempt made by the 33rd Infantry, the American division originally assigned to attack Baguio to penetrate beyond

the foothills was repelled. Moreover, and this point is very important, the U.S. 6th army believed, rightly or wrongly, as written in one of its reports "that lucrative targets were known to exist in almost every important building in Baguio, and these were therefore systematically destroyed." This statement is a justification for a policy of carpet bombing Baguio. However, I consider it a serious flaw in the U.S. Army intelligence that when the Americans started bombing the City, nobody told them—not even the guerrillas—that Yamashita was no longer in Baguio or that the City proper was not heavily defended.

2. The U.S. Army Air Forces were anxious to become a separate service and were searching for opportunities to demonstrate its capability to support ground operations.

3. The unwritten policy of Americans in warfare was the preservation of American lives. Thus, in the battle of Manila, when the Japanese decided to hold out in all the concrete structures south of the Pasig, thus, causing alarming casualties among the American soldiers, (1,000 deaths and 560 wounded) the U.S. Army decided to subject Manila, south

of the Pasig, to carpet shelling, razing that section of Manila to rubble.

These must have been the same thinking applied to the carpet bombing in Baguio. The Americans did not want high casualties resulting from street fighting in downtown Baguio as what happened in Manila.

4. It is interesting to make a comparison between Manila and Baguio in terms of the extent of destruction, both cities suffered. If you take Manila, south of the Pasig and the downtown Baguio Center, both are very comparable in the extent of the destruction suffered by both cities. Where they differ is in the scale of human casualties suffered by both cities. Manila suffered around 100,000 civilians killed caused by both the carpet shelling of the Americans in addition to the atrocities committed by the Japanese on the civilian population. In Baguio, the estimated death toll from the bombing is only around 500 to 1,000 but not more. What is important in Baguio then is not so much what happened but what did not happen. There was no madman like Admiral Iwabuchi who ordered a fight to the finish and a massacre of all the

civilians. If Yamashita had ordered a fight to the finish in Baguio, and had placed in charge someone like Iwabuchi, it could have led to a bloody massacre also.

This ends my talk on the Ordeal of Baguio.

The Guerrilla Movement

Col. Cesar P. Pobre

INTRODUCTION

DEFINITION OF TERMS

1. Guerrilla—Member of a band of irregular soldiers who wages war the unorthodox, unconventional, irregular way. It thus refers to the fighters themselves or mode of fighting (tactics and techniques) they resort to—suprise raids, ambuscades, sabotage by highly mobile, lightly armed small bands.

2. Guerrilla Movement—"connected and long-continued series of acts" undertaken by a substantial portion of the populace directly or indirectly, openly or clandestinely against

or in opposition to an unwanted civil and or military authority. It is synonymous with "underground movement."

THE JAPANESE INVASION AND OCCUPATION

1. Force: 14th Army (part of Japanese Southern Army) of two divisions (16th from Kyoto and 48th from Taiwan), plus one brigade (65th), led by Lt. Gen Masaharu Homma (w/ Lt. Gen Masami Maeda as C/S). Total Strength: around 60,000 officers and men.

2. Mission: Destroy the Phil-Am forces and seize the country in 50 days, after which the Japanese air forces and the 48th Division would be pulled out for operations in Malaya and Netherlands East Indies (Indonesia). Mission, however, was accomplished in about 150 days.

3. Bataan capitulated on 9 April, Corregidor on 6 May. But even while fighting was going on, guerrilla groups were already forming. And before long, they would be found all over the country in almost all provinces.

MOTIVATIONS OF THE GUERRILLA MOVEMENT

A. Resistance to the high-handed, oppressive tyrannical, cruel policy of the Japanese

B. Force of Filipino nationalism, sense of patriotism

C. Economic—difficult living conditions

1. Low food production, the flow of supplies was severely limited due to lack of transportation and control by the Japanese authorities, most was commandeered.

2. Manufacturing plants, shops, and business establishments were shut down or controlled.

3. Script or printed money was the medium of exchange; it was backed up and pegged to nothing; it hardly had any value. *Mickey Mouse*, it was called. The cost of commodities soared.

4. Lack of employment; many Filipino families starved.

5. Advantages of being a guerrilla:
   - Insurance from hunger
   - Having power
   - Security from guerrillas themselves

THE VARIOUS RESISTANCE GROUPS

ORGANIZERS

1. Civilian—Pre-war government officials, political leaders, or individuals of influence or leadership qualities.

2. Military—American or Filipino officers or even ordinary soldiers.

   a. Those whose units were not actually engaged in the initial stages of the invasion, thus remaining intact and not broken up. Those who did not surrender but chose to go to the hills.

   b. Those escapees from Bataan.

   c. Those who were not able to join the forces in Bataan for being cut off by the rapid Japanese advance in Central Luzon.

    d. For Americans—military or civilian—it was to avoid being interned.

THE VARIOUS GUERRILLA GROUPS

1. Luzon

   a. USAFIP-NL - Russel Volckmann

   b. LGAF (Luzon Guerrilla Army Forces) - Robert Lapham

   c. ECLGA (East Central Luzon Guerrilla Area) - Edwin Ramsey Magsaysay's Guerrillas - Ramon Magsaysay

   d. Anderson's Guerrillas
      Bulacan Military Area - Alejo Santos

   e. Hukbalahap - Luis Taruc

2. Manila Area and Southern Tagalog

   a. Hunters ROTC - Eleuterio Adevoso

   b. Marking's Fil-American Troops - Marcos Agustin

c. Fil-American Irregular Troops (FAIT) - Hugh Straughn

d. President Quezon's Own Guerrillas - Vicente Umali

e. Fil-Am Cavite Guerrillas

f. Chinese Guerrilla Groups

3. Bicol Peninsula

a. Camp Isarog's Guerrillas, Vinzon's Guerrillas, Zabat's Bicol Free Forces, Lapus' 54th Infantry, and Governor Escudero's Unit.

PROBLEM OF DISUNITY (NO UNITY OF COMMAND)

1. Geographic fragmentation

2. Difficulty of Communications

3. Personal Considerations

4. Guerrilla strategy not integrated in National Defense Plans

ACCOMPLISHMENTS

A. Raids, ambuscades, sabotage, harassing actions, mopping up operations, intelligence collection, etc.

Capture of Japanese Navy battle plan in the Central Pacific ("Z" plan for the naval defense of Marianas Island) leading to successful Battle of the Philippine Sea.

B. Psy-war efforts to counter Japanese propaganda—"guerrilla newspapers."

C. Establishment in some areas of a civil government; Areas in NL, the Visayas, and Mindanao.

D. Military operations as part of liberation campaign—role of the USAFIP-NL.

OVERALL COMMENTS

General MacArthur's strategy to defend the Philippines against Japanese invasion failed to include, as an important necessary aspect, the waging of guerrilla warfare. Which could have been resorted to not only as a fall-back position when organized conventional fighting became untenable, but as a measure to hit the Japanese forces from their rears and flanks as they raced from the beaches of Lingayen Gulf and Lamon Bay to Manila and Bataan. Examples: the North Korean Army in the Korean War and the USSR Army in WWII.

THE BATTLE OF BESSANG PASS

I was asked to write about the battle of Bessang Pass on the occasion of its 59th anniversary. I was not a participant in that great military engagement though as a military historian this much I know: it has been called "battle of the clouds."

It was so, perhaps because the sharp, steep ridges towering as high as 5,500–7,000 feet (like a row of gigantic ugly incisors pointing to the sky) that flank the Pass—and where, 59 years ago, a strong Japanese force entrenched itself for defense—are, by noon each day, shrouded with dense clouds making visibility nearly nil. Which was why, for the Northern Luzon guerrillas, Filipino freedom fighters.all, to fight and finish the enemy, capture the Pass and execute a breakthrough, they also had to battle with the clouds as they groped and inched their way up to the heights.

Bessang Pass was an important military objective. For a breakthrough at the point insured a new direction of attack (from west and north) against Japanese General Yamashita's defense perimeter. And so he could not have sensed it any less than a dagger pointing to his soft underbelly. This was why even as the battle was yet aborning he had to quickly move thousands of his troops—the crack 19th (Tora) Division—into position to defend the Pass. In so doing, that large force was pinned down and could not be withdrawn for deployment elsewhere for better advantage. Before long, it would be annihilated, and the capture of Bessang Pass would become a decisive victory for the USAFIP-NL. Decisive, because it proved to be the kind of battering ram that forced open the Japanese defense backdoor.

Victory in that battle was not only decisive, but it was also glorious, as the battle was hard—one of the most "terrible and incredibly difficult battles of the entire war" (according to the U.S. AFWESPAC Combat History Division in its book, *Triumph in the Philippines*). Moreover, it exemplified the Filipino soldier, whose resolutely fearless, intrepid, and heroic conduct in battle could only reflect the very quality of the Filipino fighting tradition.

Actually the battle of Bessang Pass was the climactic point of the dramatic role the USAFIP-NL played in the liberation campaign against the Japanese military occupation of the Philippines. The guerrilla organization grew from modest, if painful, beginnings from a handful of scattered ranks of civilians and remnants of the ill-fated Philippine Defense Force. Eventually they were all united under a single command, developing in about three years into a full division-size military outfit. Though initially thought by the landing American forces to be good only for harassing raids, sabotage, and intelligence—just like other guerrilla units—it proved to be a most effective, hard-hitting military force that worried the Japanese no end. It, in fact, waged sustained and successful combat operations against major units of the Japanese Imperial Army, a feat that perhaps other guerrilla organizations were unable to accomplish.

Even before the U.S. 6th Army could land at Lingayen, Pangasinan in early January 1945 to liberate Luzon, the USAFIP-NL had already been engaging the enemy in open combat with striking efficiency and speed. The guerrillas single-handedly liberated the west coast of Northern Luzon (the provinces of Ilocos Norte, Ilocos Sur, Abra, and La Union) save only the La Union provincial capital of San Fernando, which they cleared with American artillery and air support. Note that the area was then held by some 9,000 Japanese troops, armed to the teeth, including the first-rate Araki

Brigade. Besides, any point along its shores was a good landing place for Japanese reinforcements. There were also the Gabu airport in Laoag, Ilocos Norte, and the seaport of San Fernando winch would be staging bases for the planned Allied invasion of Japan. This was the reason U.S. 6th Army Commanding General Walter Krueger had earlier thought of sending one division to clear and hold the area. But with the liberation of this area already done by USAFIP-NL, Krueger would now plan to deploy the division he had intended for the west coast somewhere else.

It was also USAFIP-NL elements that drove the Japanese away from the areas west of the Cagayan River. This part of the Cagayan Valley was—and still is—a major producer of food crops (rice and corn, particularly). The Japanese understandably did not wish to abandon the place that would be an accessible source of supplies for the Japanese forces in Northern Luzon. But the guerrillas effectively denied them the valley, and the Japanese knew that they would die of starvation—and disease, too—and the rest of them from Fil-American bullets. Moreover, it was the USAFIP-NL's 11th and 14th Infantry troopers that inflicted heavy losses on the Japanese forces crowding in the Cagayan Valley. More importantly, the guerrillas, by relentless pressure, prevented them from joining and thus reinforcing

Yamashita's last-ditch defense in the Kiangan, Kalinga area.

Indeed, however else the USAFIP-NL's role in the victorious war against Japan may be assessed, it is worth noting that only 3 U.S. army divisions with a total strength of 60,000 were assigned to fight at any one time 120,000–180,000 Japanese defense forces in the mountain fastnesses of Northern Luzon, where American mechanized forces—their competitive edge had but limited application. To match the enemy man for man and insure his destruction and ultimate defeat, MacArthur would have been compelled to throw into the fray 3 additional divisions. He did not have to, however, because of the presence and effective participation of the 20,000 strong USAFIP-NL in the fighting.

Although the fighting cost the USAFIP-NL 5,000 of its men, it exacted mere than 50,000 casualties from the enemy. If that, was a satisfying outcome, it was even mere so when one day—a great day to be sure for the guerrillas—General Yamashita would show up personally before the USAFIP-NL command to turn in his forces formally in keeping with the formal surrender of Japan on 1 September 1945. Some 33,011 Japanese officers and men · surrendered to the USAFIP-NL, including a number of generals and admirals, like Rear

Admiral Kyoguro Simamato, commander of a submarine division that attacked Pearl Harbor.

If all this is enough credit, it must be shared by the people of Northern Luzon upon whose sacrifices and support the USAFIP-NL depended for its very life and success.

Personal Experience

Fr. James B. Reuter, S.J.

When the war started, on 8 December 1941, I was
teaching Sophomore A.B. in the Ateneo de Manila on
Padre Faura. That day, the Feast of the Immaculate
Conception, was a holiday because the Virgin Mary
was the Patroness of the Ateneo. The whole school
was decorated with banners and bunting. We had a
local band, playing in the school courtyard, since early
morning.

Most of the students, and all of us teachers, were
gathered in the new theater, built by Father Henry Lee
Irwin, for Mass, when word came about the bombing of
Pearl Harbor, then the bombing of Clark Air Base, and
finally the bombing of Baguio.

The students were in a state of panic. All the boarders
went home. Classes stopped. There was no more school. I
was 25 years old at that time, a young Jesuit seminarian

in regency, not yet ordained. We, the Scholastics, had no expectations at all that this war was going to break over us. We did not expect that it would last a long time. But our superiors did.

They were incredibly wise on the analysis of how long this war would last. On 9 December, the next day, we began to be rationed. We were hungry for the next three years and three months. The smaller men survived a little better than the big ones, because we were all given the same amount of food.

The U.S. Army threw open their *bodegas*. They gave away everything, not charging anybody. Most of the Filipinos went for the beef, the slaughtered pigs, the canned goods. But our Jesuit Superiors went to the bodega in a truck and they took nothing but barrels of wine and sacks of flour. Only that. Nothing else. And the result was: for the next three years and three months we had Mass, every day.

From 9 December the Jesuit priests began to say Mass with a small host. When we received Communion, it was a fragment of a small host. As altar boys, we put the wine into the chalice with an eyedropper, and the water with an eyedropper.

Father Hurley, our Superior, gave wine and flour to all the religious who asked for it. He never refused anyone. It was a blessing.

The Ateneo at Padre Faura became a refugee center. We wound up with about 460 refugees. They lived in all the classrooms, sleeping on the floor. One night an Inter-Island boat, the Corregidor, overloaded with students from the provinces trying to get home, hit one of our mines in Manila Bay and went down. We got the survivors, on stretchers, terribly burned, covered with oil. They became part of the refugees.

We had all kinds of people in our compound. Mostly American families, several Jews who had fled from Austria, and four missionaries who were on their way to India, from the Congregation of the Holy Cross. Their ship was bombed in Manila Bay. They were with us for the next three years, the duration of the war.

Because we did not have enough food, we began to dig up our playing fields, and plant. We planted *pechay*, because *pechay* will grow anywhere. When we dug into the earth, at a depth of 12 inches we found sand, seashells, and salt water! The ground on which the Ateneo was built was re-filled!

The Japanese bombed at will, with absolutely no opposition. Manila was an open city. The only time we saw an American plane was just after a Japanese bombing. The American plane would be flying low over the city, trying to get out.

The Japanese bombings got stronger and stronger as the month of December went on. When they bombed we would be down on the floor, because the whole building would rock. But by the third bomb you could tell what their target was. They would bomb in a figure 8. When they crossed the center of the 8, the bomb would fall. They would circle, and as they crossed the center of the 8, boom! Another bomb. Many planes, all aiming at the same target.

The Church of Santo Domingo was bombed. At that time it was downtown, close to the Pasig River. The Japanese were really aiming at the shipping in the Pasig. When they missed by 50 meters, they hit Santo Domingo Church. Our emotional radio broadcasters went wild over this. They said: "The Japanese have said they were only bombing military targets! Yesterday they bombed Santo Domingo. Was the Church of Santo Domingo a military target? One bomb fell on the Blessed Virgin Mary. Was the Virgin Mary a military target?"

We sang Christmas carols in all the hospitals. The young Jesuit Scholastics, all male voices. The American hospitals were so desolate! We knew that things were pretty bad because the Americans left in the city were so depressed!

Father Horacio de la Costa had written a beautiful book on the history of the Jesuits in the Philippines, from 1859 until 1941. That book was due to come out at Christmas time. All the printed copies were stacked up in the Good Shepherd Press. The press was bombed. Most of the books were destroyed. A few copies were saved. The book was reprinted only in 1995.

The Japanese took us at midnight, on 1 January 1942. They were outside the city all day long, but they did not want to enter the city in the daytime because of the snipers. They came in when it was dark. At midnight they were on Padre Faura, between U.P. and the Ateneo, cheering, shouting, singing. They came into our compound, opened every door, and looked at us. We did not get out of bed. But the Japanese moved on, from room to room. They did not want trouble at that time.

In the morning, when we woke up, they had sandbags piled across the front gate, with soldiers lying behind the sandbags, with rifles. From that moment, we were internees—civilian prisoners of war. For the 460 of us there were 4 red armbands. The red armband would allow you to go out, to buy food, or medicine, or see a doctor.

The religious section of the Japanese occupying forces came in with the third wave. They brought in Japanese nuns—very dignified, reverent, edifying. They would kneel in the Cathedral at Mass very prayerfully, not moving for a full hour. I did not see any Japanese priests, but they had many seminarians.

One seminarian came to visit us Jesuit Scholastics at Padre Faura. He did not know any English, and we did not know any Japanese. But in those days all of our studies in Philosophy and Theology were in Latin.

So he sat down on the bed with us, in our dormitory, and we talked in Latin. We could understand each other perfectly. Clear as a bell! It was fiercely interesting. He was on the water, offshore of the Philippines, in October of 1941! The war did not hit us until 8 December. And he was in the third wave! We wondered why the United States never knew about that.

During the first three months of 1942 we were listening to the Voice of Freedom, a radio broadcast from the American forces on Corregidor. We listened at night, with all the fights out, in the dark, with the radio tuned very low. If the Japanese caught anyone listening to the Voice of Freedom, they were "dealt with severely." This was their term for handing you over to the *Kempeitai* in Fort Santiago.

In the beginning, the Voice of Freedom was Leon Maria Guerrero, an Ateneo alumnus, the star in our "Commonwealth Hour"—the Catholic Hour of the Philippines. He stopped announcing for fear that harm would come to his family, and then Norman Reyes became the Voice of Freedom.

Then came that terrible day, in April, when Bataan fell. The Voice of Freedom was silent. Instead, we heard the voice of General Skinny Wainwright. He sounded so tired, so depressed, so beaten. He was on all the radio stations, but even if you shut off the radio, you could still hear him. There was no escape. The Japanese had loudspeakers set up at every street corner. Wainwright was saying, in his weary, defeated voice: "I am speaking to our soldiers in Northern Luzon. The American Forces in the Philippines have surrendered. Please lay down your arms!.... and now I am speaking to our soldiers in Mindanao. We have surrendered to the Japanese. Please—I beg of you—lay down your arms!"

It was the saddest night of the war.

Then came the Death March. Many of our schoolboys were in the Death March because from 8th December, the ROTC cadets began training for real war. They practiced with real guns, real bullets, and real hand grenades. Then they went out to Bataan, when they did not have to go. They went as volunteers.

They stayed in Bataan for three months, with very little ammunition, with almost no food, with nothing but courage. They were saying to each other, "How terrible it would be if we surrender tonight, and the Americans came tomorrow morning!" They thought the Americans were steaming across the Pacific Ocean in battleships, to save them. But they weren't.

So they were in the Death March. One mother knew the path they were taking, so she went out there, trying to see her son. She was relatively young, and her hair was black. When she saw her son, her hair turned white. And it stayed white for the rest of her life.

In the prison camp at Capas, they were dying 50 a day. They were being buried in long trenches, 50 at a time, with no I.D., no identifying mark. When they dug up the bodies, after the war, they never knew who was who.

In the big beautiful American cemetery in Fort Bonifacio they have all the names on the walls, and 36,000 white crosses, with a body under every cross. But they do not know which body is under which cross.

There was magnificent heroism in those days. Benito Soliven was a Congressman, a Major in the Reserves. He went to Bataan when he did not have to go. He was in the Death March and was very sick in Capas.

He was offered his freedom if he would join the puppet government. He said, "No. If I did that, I would have to compromise. And, in conscience, I can't do that. I'll get out of this prison camp when everybody else gets out."

He was an honest man. He ran for Congress in Ilocos, against Elpidio Quirino. He defeated Quirino so badly that Quirino withdrew from politics. It was Quezon who brought Quirino back, because Quirino was Quezon's white-haired boy. Just before the war broke, late in November of 1941, Benito Soliven was the speaker, in Tondo, to all the men in the Procession of Christ the King. He was not only honest, and brave. He was close to God.

When finally he was released from Capas, he was so sick that he died. We buried him from the Paco Church. He had ten children, and the tenth—the baby—died before he did, of malaria and malnutrition.

A battalion of Japanese was based in a school, on the corner of Taft Avenue and Padre Faura. Their compound was surrounded by a barbed wire fence. When they ate, they sat on the ground, in an open area, completely visible to the hungry Filipinos, who lined up outside the barbed wire, looking at them. Embarrassed by this, the Japanese set up a *sawali* fence inside the barbed wire fence, so that they would not be seen when they were eating.

They put up the *sawali* fence late one afternoon. The next morning, to their amazement, the barbed wire fence was gone—stolen by the Filipinos!

The war was agony, in many ways, but it also revealed stark heroism. One of the students in my class at the Ateneo was Ramon Cabrera. He was the left half of the football team. That team was undefeated, untied, unscored upon. They won the NCAA championship on 7 December, and the war broke the next day. Cabrera went into training with the ROTC, went to Bataan, was in the Death March, and in the prison camp at Capas. He was not big, but he was in good physical shape. He survived. Released from Capas, he went into the Underground.

And the Japanese picked him up and brought him to Fort Santiago. There, they wanted him to give the names of his friends who were with him in the Underground. Cabrera said: "I don't know any names."

To make him talk, they beat him in the mouth with a gun butt. They broke all his teeth. They smashed the jaw. They smashed the nose. But still, he would not talk. So they brought him to the cemetery, gave him a shovel, and said: "Dig your own grave!" Cabrera said: "Dig it yourself!" so they bayoneted him. He dropped to his knees, looked up at the guard who bayoneted him and smiled. It was a strange smile because he was bubbling blood, and the blood was black.

But even when he fell, you could tell who was the winner. The Japanese had to dig the grave themselves.

He was only a Filipino schoolboy—Sophomore A.B. But greater love than this no man hath, that he lay down his life for his friends. When the pressure is on, that is when the great virtues of the Filipino come to the surface!

After we had been interned in the Ateneo for about a year, the Japanese decided that they wanted to use the place. So we were driven out, with all of our refugees. The Jesuits went to two different places. Those of us who were studying Theology went to the Paulist Seminary on San Marcelino Street. We were housed on the top floor of what is now Adamson University. The others went to La Ignaciana, on Herran Street in Santa Ana. We transferred on foot, bringing all the things we needed in push carts—bedding, clothing, books.

The young Jesuits were deeply resentful of the Japanese. We did not like being thrown out of our own school, our own house. So some of the Scholastics began to remove all the fixtures from the shower rooms.

They removed the door knobs, the faucets, the electric lights. And when the Japanese discovered this, they were furious!

And then, while we were gathering the things we had to take with us, we found two boxes of bayonets! They were part of the equipment of the ROTC. We never meant to conceal them from the Japanese. But they were buried under other equipment in a corner of the ROTC store room, and we did not know they were there!

Father Mickey Keane, S.J., the Jesuit in charge, was afraid to declare them to the Japanese at that moment, because they were so angry! They might execute a couple of Jesuits for conspiracy. So he put the bayonets on one of the pushcarts, covered them with bedding and clothing. We pushed the whole cartload to La Ignaciana.

Father Kennally, the Jesuit in charge at La Ignaciana, was very nervous about possessing those bayonets. So he wrote a note to Father Keane, saying: "What shall we do with the bayonets?" He gave this note to Jaime Neri, a Scholastic, to deliver. And Neri was picked up by the Japanese! They found the note!

Meantime, Father Kennally made his own decision. He opened the boxes and threw the bayonets, one by one, into the Pasig River...And then the Japanese appeared, asking: "Where are the bayonets?" Father Kennally told the truth, that he had thrown them into the river. So the Japanese took the Jesuit Scholastics, tied each one around the waist with a rope, and made them dive into the Pasig, to recover the bayonets.

One of the Scholastics was Freddie Escaler, who later became a bishop He said: "We were tied with a rope, not to keep us from drowning, but to keep us from swimming away! We did not find a single bayonet because the mud in the Pasig River was 18 inches deep! The bayonets were buried in the mud!"

This event caused many Jesuits to be hauled into Fort Santiago: Fathers Keane, Kennally, Hurley, Mulry. And Jaime Neri. Father Mulry was released after some months, because the Japanese discovered that he had raised money for Japan after one of their terrible earthquakes. Father Mulry, released, walked to San Ignacio, the Jesuit Church in Intramuros.

The Jesuit community welcomed him, and fed him at once, because he was almost starved. After he had eaten, Father Mulry said to the Community, who were listening eagerly: "Thomas à Kempis says: *'Cellula continuata dulcescit.'* Your little cell, if you stay in it long enough, becomes sweet!... I want to tell you, Brothers... It's a damn lie!"

The prisoners of war—the American soldiers—were treated very badly. They had a much harder time than we did. But every once in a while a truckload of prisoners would go by our quarters on San Marcelino, and they would wave to us with the victory sign. So we waved back, with the victory sign. This made the Spanish Paules very angry. They called us: "Los Caballeros Americanos," and said "You will get us all into trouble!"

But when the Japanese moved the Jesuit Scholastics to San Agustin, all of the Paulist priests were bayoneted and their bodies were thrown into the *estero*. And they were Spanish! They were not even at war with the Japanese!

In the middle of their Occupation, the Japanese gave Independence to the Philippines. The puppet President was Jose Laurel, and he was the speaker on that day, in the Luneta. He knew his business! He began speaking in English, with all the Japanese sitting in front of him with their samurai swords.

He said: "I am accused of being a puppet of the Japanese. But I am a puppet of no man! And I say this to the Japanese, to their teeth! ...I am president of this country so that I can help my people!" Then he threw away the English speech he had prepared, and broke into Tagalog. The people cheered. And the Japanese smiled. He was saying exactly what they wanted him to say.

Then Aguinaldo brought out the Filipino flag. Aguinaldo never surrendered to the Americans. He raised the flag himself. The Jesuit Filipino Scholastics came home in tears, deeply moved. It was the first time they had ever seen the Filipino flag go up alone.

When the Americans returned, they gave Independence to the Philippines, in 1946. The Filipinos, who smile and laugh at everything, had their own little joke about this. They said: "Now we have Japanese Independence, and we have American Independence. The Swedes want to come and give us Swedish Independence!"

The Japanese decided that they wanted the Paulist Seminary, so they threw us out, and transferred us to the Monastery of San Agustin, in Intramuros. Then one evening they herded us all into the dining room, where they conducted a head count. They were preparing to move us to Los Baños, on the next day.

There was one Jesuit Scholastic missing—Big Ed McGinty. He was sick, in the hospital. Actually it was starvation. He died, later. But at San Agustin our Jesuit superior, Father Francis Dowling Burns, was trying to cover for him. He did not want the Japanese to take him. So he was telling vague, various stories of the whereabouts of Big Ed McGinty.

The Japanese Officer in charge had an interpreter. He was getting all this by interpretation. But suddenly he grew very angry and said in excellent idiomatic English: "You're giving us the run-around! Where is he?" He knew English perfectly, but he was using the interpreter so we would not know that he could understand every small side remark that anyone made.

Horacio de la Costa was very pale at that time, because he recognized the Japanese Officer. He had seen him, in Fort Santiago, beating a prisoner with a wire whip.

The trucks came at four in the morning, to take us to Los Baños. But they took us first to the University of Santo

Tomas, where they kept us for one day, in the gym. We slept on the floor.

Father Frank McSorley, O.M.I. was one of the internees who were concentrated in UST. His blood brother, Dick McSorley, S.J. was one of us Jesuit Scholastics. There were fifteen children in the McSorley family. Five of the boys became priests, and three of the girls became nuns. ...Frank came to the gym, hoping to talk to his brother, but the Japanese guard stopped him about ten meters from the entrance. Dick came to the door. Frank was arguing with the guard, but looking over the guard's shoulder, at his brother. At least they saw each other! Frank later became the first Bishop of Jolo.

In the morning we took the train to Los Baños. With the Jesuits were all of the religious officials, ministers, pastors of the countries that were at war with Japan. All of the Catholic priests and seminarians were in Barracks 19. The Catholic nuns were in Barracks 20. The La Salle Brothers were in Barracks 17. The Protestants, Seventh Day Adventists, Lutherans, Baptists were in other barracks.

Each barracks was like an Indian Long House—a dirt floor running down the middle, a bamboo floor raised about six inches from the ground on both sides, the whole area divided by thin *sawali* walls, making cubicles for about six people. Each barracks had sixteen cubicles, so we were about 96 internees in every barracks. We, the newcomers, were separated from the internees who were already there, in the campus of U.P. Los Baños. They called us "Vatican City."

The Japanese did not know what to do with the Anglicans. Leading the Anglicans was a young pastor named Walter Damrasch III, the grandson of the famous conductor of the Philadelphia Symphony Orchestra. The Anglicans did not want to be billeted with the Protestants. Walter Damrasch said: "We are Catholics! There are three branches of the Catholic Faith—Roman, English, and Middle East. We are a branch of the Catholic Faith!"

When the Japanese questioned the Jesuits about the Anglicans, Father Francis Dowling Burns said: "They are Protestants!" So the Anglicans stayed in a field, under the blazing sun, for three hours, while the Japanese were deciding what to do with them. Finally, a ranking Japanese Officer came to Damrasch and asked: "Do you have wives?" Damrasch said: "Yes... but, you see..." and the Japanese Officer said: "Protestant!" They were billeted among the Protestants.

There was no hostility among the different religions, in that camp. We all accepted each other, completely.

We were united by a common enemy, and by a common desire—survival! For instance, the Seventh Day Adventists had a handsaw, which they would not use on Saturday, their Sabbath Day. There was no furniture in the Barracks. If you wanted a chair, you had to build it. So every Saturday the Jesuits would borrow the saw of the Seventh Day Adventists.

The Anglicans were very close to the Catholics. If you saw them saying Mass, you would think it was a Catholic ceremony. The only difference was the language. The Anglican Ministers said the Mass in English. The Catholic priests said the Mass in Latin. In all other things, we were the same. We never had any disputes about doctrine. We felt that we were one—all children of the same God.

The Japanese told us that they would give us a certain amount of self-government. We should elect a Central Committee of 15 members. So we had elections. Many of the internees carried on real campaigns. In the final 15, eight were British. The other seven came from different countries. Our own Father Francis Dowling Burns was elected. All men. No women.

When the elections were over, the 15 men presented themselves to Konichi, the Japanese who was running the camp. They said: "We are the Central Committee.

What are our rights and obligations?" Konichi said: "If anyone tries to escape from this camp, we will execute you 15."... The Central Committee came back to us, each one to his own barracks, saying: "Please, don't try to break out of this camp! The Americans will come! Sooner or later, they will come! Please don't try to escape!" It was the smartest thing the Japanese could have done, to maintain discipline in the camp.

Father Mulry died in the prison camp. He was really killed in Fort Santiago. There, sitting on the floor, facing the wall, for three months, he developed stomach ulcers. One night, in our barracks, he threw up a tremendous amount of blood. Al Grau, our infirmarian, bent over him as he was lying on the floor in a pool of his blood, and said: "Father, how do you feel?" Father Mulry said: "Oh, I feel so much better now!" I guess the blood had been building up in his stomach.

We carried him down to our little hospital, on a door. We got the door when the Japanese abandoned a little house and allowed the internees to tear it apart for the wood. We were growing *pechay* around every Barracks, and we needed the wood to cook the *pechay*. The Jesuits took the door. For Father Mulry, we used it as a stretcher.

In that little hospital, they had no medicine. The only doctor was Doctor Nance, who was a surgeon, a former

Protestant missionary in China. The only way he could find out what was wrong with a patient was by operating on him. As they prepared for the operation he was walking around in *chinelas* and shorts. No shirt. He had one cigarette. He lit it, took a deep puff on it, and shared it with the American Navy nurse. There was only one Navy nurse on duty in the hospital that night. The nurses for Father Mulry's operation were Maryknoll nuns.

Father Greer went to Father Mulry and gave him three cigarettes, which were very precious at that time. Father Mulry said: "Oh, I wouldn't need all that many!" He died on the operating table. Doctor Nance put his hand through the incision and pumped the heart with his fingers, but it didn't work.

We carried him back, on the same door, to the chapel. In the morning we had Mass. The nuns were tiptoeing up to the altar, to look at the body, to find out who it was. They did not even know that Father Mulry was sick. After the Mass, we buried him in our little cemetery.

When we buried the first internee in that cemetery we really dug down six feet. But, as the months went by, we got weaker, and the graves became shallower—5 feet... 4 feet... 3 feet... 2 feet. Father Mulry was the 18th. So, with his grave, we just covered the top of our makeshift coffin with about six inches of soil.

One morning we heard a rifle shot just before dawn. No one was allowed out of their barracks at night. We went to the door of our Barracks and looked out. Just outside the first row of barbed wire was a young American Pan Am flier, rolling on the ground, shot through the shoulder. He was holding a bundle. Konichi stood over the body and said: "It's a military offense to try to escape from this camp! Even if he were not shot, we would execute him!" So they dragged the body out to a little gully and put a bullet through his head. We heard the shot.

When they gave us the body, the bullet hole was small in the back and big in the front. It blew out all the brains. When we were burying him, I said to another member of the burial crew, who was also a Pan Am flier: "What was he trying to do, breaking out at dawn?"

Because we had three rows of barbed wire surrounding that camp and four rows of Japanese guards. And they were incredible shots. You could never make it out of that camp, through the barbed wire, at dawn!

The Pan Am boy said: "He was not shot trying to get out! He was shot trying to get back in!" He got out, about midnight. But then he found food—bananas, a coconut, and rice. He thought of his wife and baby, who was born in that camp. So he was trying to get back in. If he had five minutes more, he would have made it. But just at that time, there was a small streak of light. The guards saw him and shot him. We buried him in a shallow grave.

The Japanese thought that he had brought the bundle from inside the camp. Supplies for his journey. So they gave it to us. We gave it to his wife. The rice was soaked with his blood.

When we saw the American planes flying over the camp, on their way to bombing Manila, we knew that the end was coming. We could tell that they were American planes because of the way they sounded. Very smooth. The Japanese planes sounded like a washing machine. And the American planes were white. They really gave us high hopes.

While we were in that camp, the young Jesuits became the entertainers. We wrote about 24 songs while we were there. Parodies. We would take an existing song and put our own words to it. This is one of them:

> What is the hope that the white planes bring?
> What puts the zip in the songs we sing?
>> What's the reason for...
>> The crowd round the Barracks door?

Why do you thrill at the boom of guns?
Why do you dream of cinnamon buns?
 It is the certainty...
 That some day we will be free

Ah! You have things to get you down...

To make you fret and to make you frown...
 You're locked up, but you'll be free...
 You darned old internee!

Heigh, ho, the merry oh...
 You'll be happy as can be!
Too bad for Tokyo...
 It was such a nice city!

You'll sail the sea, across the foam...
The band will play when you come home...

 You'll be glad you used to be
 A darned old internee!
Ah.... You darned all internee!

We even sang about Konichi. We couldn't say his name, because the Japanese would understand. So we substituted "Da Dee Dee" Konichi lived in Barracks Three. So we sang:

Who's the boy
Fills us all with joy?
Clever, kind, and coy...
　　Da Dee Dee!

Lives in Three
Bosses you and me...
We'll hang him from a tree!
　　Da Dee Dee!

Your starvation causes him no pain...
Why if our Army wasn't here he'd do it once again!

In 90 hours
That boy will be ours...
We'll put him in the cawas...
　　Oh Dee Dee rah, rah, rah!
　　Oh, Da Dee Dee rah, rah, rah!
　　Oh, Da Dee Dee rah, rah, rah,
　　　　rah, rah, rah, rah!

We sang that around a fireside, at night. The internees loved it. The Japanese guards were listening, but they did not understand.

The paratroopers of the Eleventh Airborne dropped on us on 23 February 1945. At 7:00 o'clock, when the first parachute opened, the *guerrilleros* began to fire from outside the camp. They had been lying there, all night, waiting. Their bullets were whizzing through our barracks. So we lay down flat, on the bamboo floor.

The Japanese came running through our barracks, firing at the *guerrilleros* through our windows. The raid was beautifully timed. Most of our Japanese guards were doing their morning exercise, which they called "Radio Taiso."And their guns were stacked! Our 211 guards were killed in fifteen minutes.

The first American soldier that I saw was a big black boy who came to the door of our Barracks and said: "If y'all would get out into the road... we're gonna evacuate you folks in a little while!" It was such a beautiful feeling! Some of the Maryknoll Sisters were so exhilarated that they wrapped their arms around the first American soldier they saw, and kissed him! One American boy took off his helmet, in the middle of the battle, and said: "Gee! This is the nicest battle I ever been in!"

Then the great amtracks came up from Laguna de Bay, and smashed over the barbed wire into our camp. They put the internees into these amtracks. Some of the internees, who hated the Japanese because of the long years of imprisonment, were dragging the dead bodies of the Japanese into the path of the amtracks, so that the tanks would crush them.

But most of the American soldiers had never seen a Japanese before. This was their first face to face contact with them. They had not suffered as much as the internees. So the drivers of the amtracks would never crush a body. When they saw a dead Japanese in front of them, their tank would stop, rear up like a horse, turn, and go around the body.

When we reached Laguna de Bay those great heavy tanks rolled right into the water. They were amphibious! They sailed across the bay like a ship. The Japanese were firing at us from the hills. One of my friends, Pete Leary, was standing in the amtrack, looking over the side. The water was dancing up and down. Leary said: "Look at the fish!" But the American manning the machine gun on top of our tank said: "That's not fish! Those are machine gun bullets!" So we all crouched down in the body of the amtracks until the American planes silenced the Japanese machine guns.

The amtracks landed at Calamba. From there they took us in trucks to Muntinglupa, to New Bilibid Prison. They chose the prison because it was surrounded by high stone walls. The war was still on, and the Americans were fighting off the Japanese from the prison walls. Our supplies were dropped us by planes.

At that time, the Americans were not taking prisoners. Even if a Japanese came out naked, with his hands up, they would shoot him dead. Because too many Japanese had pretended to surrender, but they were carrying hand grenades under their armpits. They were willing to die so long as they blew up the Americans. The Japanese soldiers had said to us, very clearly: "We can never surrender! We can never surrender!"

At Muntinglupa we were weighed by the Red Cross. Joe Maxey, a Jesuit Scholastic, started the war on 8 December 1941 at 240 pounds. When he was weighed at Muntinglupa, three years and three months later, he weighed 118. He had lost more than half his weight during those three years. But it happened so gradually that we did not even notice it.

Tommy Thompson started the war at 220. When he was liberated, he weighed 100 pounds, flat. We looked like skeletons, but we did not realize it, at the time. We lost a number of men, in the year that followed the war. Charlie Riley, in his twenties, died of a heart attack. Mike Cashman, whose father fought for the light heavyweight championship of the world, died in New York six months after liberation. When we lost men like this, the doctors said: "Well, you have to expect that... the stress and strain takes its toll."

Manila was liberated at the same time as we were. It was strange—the American La Salle brothers were with us in the prison camp at Los Baños, and they all survived. But the German La Salle Brothers, who were allies of the Japanese, and the Irish Brothers, who were not at war with Japan, were all killed!

La Salle College was filled with refugees. When the Americans were closing in on them, the Japanese did not want to have anyone behind them. So they gathered all the men, including the Brothers, and bayoneted them. They did not want to waste bullets on the refugees. They were saving the bullets for the Americans.

Then they took the women and raped them, from the youngest to the oldest, many times. Then they bayoneted them. Some of the poor girls were bayoneted through the genitals. They left the bodies in the chapel. The siege went on, their lust came back, and some of the Japanese soldiers came into the chapel, turning over the bodies of the girls, looking for someone who was still alive, so that they could rape her again. That cold-blooded massacre was pretty bad. And there were many like that.

But some good things did happen. Konichi was condemned for war crimes. One of his crimes was starving us. A second crime was the massacre of Calamba. When he was on trial, he asked to be instructed in the Catholic Faith. So this was done until he was convicted. He was suffering from TB. They hurried the trial because they did not want him to die a natural death.

On the day of his execution, they carried him down to the gallows, in the same place where we were imprisoned, the pig pen of U.P. Los Baños! It was four o'clock in the morning. The priest baptized him at the foot of the gallows. He did not even have to go to confession, because he was not a Catholic. Baptism remits all the guilt of sin.

The priest then stood under the gallows. The trapdoor opened, and Konichi fell, his hands tied behind his back. The priest anointed his hands. This means that Konichi went straight to heaven, without even a stop over in Purgatory!

We, the Jesuits who were imprisoned at Los Baños, believe that this happened because the nuns were praying for Konichi. Almost all of the internees hated him. One said: "I would gladly give my life, if only I could get Konichi." But the nuns prayed that God would be merciful to him. And God heard their prayers!

The most touching story of the whole war, for me, was the story of Captain Okanu, of the Japanese religious section. We met him this way. One of our refugees at Padre Faura was Mrs. Lippy. Her husband was a military man who was killed in the first bombings of the war. Mrs. Lippy was living in one of our Ateneo classrooms, with three other families. With her were her four children, and a Filipina maid, who was their *yaya*.

Mrs. Lippy told the maid never to pass near the front gate, where the Japanese were. But one day there was no water, except in one tap. The maid went to that tap, to get water, passing the front gate. A Japanese Lieutenant saw her, and said: "You will come back here at 8 o'clock tonight."

Frightened, the maid told this to Mrs. Lippy, who told it to Father Hurley, our Jesuit Superior. Father Hurley went to the classroom and stood in front of the door. When the girl did not appear, the Japanese came to get her. Father Hurley said: "I am the Superior here, and these are my guests. I must protect them."

The Japanese slapped him, hard, again and again. Then he began to beat him with his sword. Father Hurley was over six feet and could have broken the Japanese in two, but he never raised his hands. Father Russel Sullivan, meantime, had called the religious section of the Japanese. Captain Okanu came. He outranked the

Lieutenant. It ended with the Lieutenant bowing to Father Hurley and saying: "So sorry! So sorry! So sorry!"

From then on, Captain Okanu was our friend. Even when we were in Los Baños, he helped us in many ways. Once he showed Father Greer a picture of his wife. He said: "I am the only Catholic in my family. My wife became a Catholic when we were married. We were married only two weeks when I was sent to the Philippines."

Then he said to Father Greer: "Soon you free... Me dead." Father Greer said: "Ah, no! If you surrender, you will be free. It is only a matter of time." But Okanu said: "No. I could never surrender. If I surrendered, I could not live in Japan." ...Okanu did not surrender. And he was killed.

A full year later, when Father Greer was on his way back to the Philippines after being repatriated, he stopped in Tokyo. He was so grateful to Okanu that he wanted to visit his family, and tell them how good the Captain was. He had the address, but when he found the place, it was flat—destroyed by the American bombing. He sounded around, and found a man who said: "Yes! But they moved!" He gave a new address.

Father Greer traveled across Tokyo, a city he did not know, and found the second address. But it was a store.

The storekeeper said: "Yes! They used to live here, but they moved!" He gave a third address. Father Greer finally found Okanu's home.

The family sat on the floor, enraptured, while he spoke. They had heard nothing about their son. Not a word. Father Greer was trying to remember every good thing he knew about the Captain. All the family had become Catholics, individually, one by one, each for his own personal reasons. But he could not see any wife.

Finally he brought out her picture. The effect was electric. All of they said: "Oh, you must see her! You must see her!" So they all dressed and led him up and down through narrow streets and alleys until they came to a big house. They rang the bell. A girl answered. They spoke in Japanese. The girls ushered Father Greer into a little parlor, while the family stayed outside.

A nun came to the door of the parlor. Father Greer said: "I am looking for the wife of Captain Okanu." The nun smiled, and said: "I am Mrs. Okanu." She had been educated in a Catholic school and wanted to become a nun since she was in college, but her family would not allow her even to become a Catholic. Until they arranged the wedding with this young officer whom they liked. Her family allowed her to become a Catholic just before she married him. After two weeks, he was sent to the

Philippines, and there he was killed. So then she entered the convent—the Handmaids of the Sacred Heart.

Later, I met this nun in Japan. She was a very kind, gentle soul. She came to the Philippines, to see where her husband served his country, and his people, as a Japanese should. He gave his life for his country. And at the same time was a blessing to the people with whom Japan was at war.

The war was a great adventure. I learned many things. God never lets anything happen to you, unless he can draw it into good.

Thank you for listening, and God bless you all!

Economic Life During the Japanese Occupation: Civilian Support for the Resistance Movement

Gloria M. Santos

Little did I know that this day would be one of the heaviest days in my 83 years of life. I did not know that the husband of my beloved secretary is more than a secretary to me because she is not supposed to be a secretary in the first place. She's our guidance counselor, time management officer of St. Mary's College. She lost her husband through a heart attack Monday morning. And Monday evening, I woke up, I was told that he died and the burial was Tuesday, this morning and naturally, I have to be present, if at all, at the mass, which is to be celebrated by the way in Greenmeadows. And you know between here and Greenmeadows, the distance, and the traffic. But as if it was not enough, I forgot that today is the 50th anniversary of the International Christian Leadership. Do you know what International Christian Leadership is? It is a gathering of Congressmen, Senators, and Government Officials in Washington D.C. It is one of the beloved agencies which was established here by the American forces when they came in. It was Ambassador Fergusson who brought the chapter here. And since it is an ecumenical gathering, the Roman Catholic Faith has to have representatives. Cardinal Santos who was then the president of the Bishop's Conference, the CBCP. At the same time, Archbishop of Manila designated eight people, among them, I was the only lady member, the rest were bishops. All of them have gone to heaven except Monsignor Ortiz and myself. Well, according to Dr. Pobre, I will not be answering the roll call for a long time. Its that every time St. Peter calls the roll, he answers for me "absent." And so he says, he doesn't expect me to join the happy crowd over there. So with that said, I have to be there, because I am the only representative now remaining in that group or the Roman Catholics to speak for our church by the mandate of the Bishops.

When Cardinal Sin took over, I was asking to be relieved but he said that he will only relieve me from that position if I promise to say mass everyday and take confession, which means I have to take the place of one priest because, the ratio of our Roman Catholic priests is now, if you will permit me, is 32,000 faithfuls to one Roman Catholic priest. And you can imagine how heavily loaded the priests are. I cannot do both, I cannot give confession and I cannot have the honor of celebrating the Eucharist. I have to be contented with representing our church. So I went there at 6:30 in the morning, begged all of the indulgences of that group, mainly Protestants, pastors and what have you. I said my little message and then I went to Green meadows to catch up with the mass of my beloved Elaine for her husband and I begged off to sleep quietly so that I can catch up with this. I never thought I would have this hectic day in my 83 years of life. But having said that, let me pick up from where our immediate speaker has left off—that's the slaughter of civilians. I would call it slaughter, no less. I can think of no other word. I really cannot, and I would not want to talk about anything about the war. It is so painful to me. The pain is so great I can hardly bear it. However, it is my love for NHI that made me accept this, and I confided to our Philippine Historical Association (PHA) president, Dr. Evelyn Miranda. I lost almost all of my friends in that terrible holocaust. Imagine, young teenagers, ages 17, 18, 19—16, yes 16, being herded off to Bataan and Corregidor from the campuses of their respective universities. Not even knowing because you know what the ROTC is, it is a big joke, you must know.

It is a contest of muses. You want to be an officer because you want to bring your ladylove there in the rostrum, dance with her during the cadet ball. You know I can see my good friend Benito Legarda laughing his head off because maybe he is one of those cadets. They did not even know where the end of the rifle begins, and where it ends. And most of the time what they are carrying are not real guns, they are wooden guns. And they have to parade all over the ground, pretending they are military people when they don't even read their manual. One of my dear friends, supposedly a commanding officer of the ROTC Cadet Corps, thought that the duty officer, when the Cadet Corps is attacked has to lead his group out. He did not know that the officer of the day, when the camp is attacked, is suppose to stay, save all the documents, burn all of those that will harm the cause and salvage whatever ammunitions he can. But he is under pain of court martial to leave his post. But that's what he did. He led his army out of the camp and started running for dear life. He did not know that the OD has to stay on duty. That's why he is called the officer on duty. Of course, he was not court-martialed because he was a young cadet of 16 or 17 years old. I'm talking of one of your alumni here in UST, Dr. Hector Santos who has passed away already.

From that part, the first days of the war, he served the medical corps faithfully, seeing how his colleagues were killed at his side. That's only one of those things.

Talking of the Pasig River, I wonder if our colleagues, ever discovered why there is so much theater in those days. It was because many of the Filipinos civilians were listening to the Voice of America. And the Voice of America was broadcasting even on the day before 3rd February, that of the entry of the American troops would take place from the north, I mean from the south. That is Leyte. I mean General MacArthur landed in Leyte, so they would be coming in, and they would enter Manila by the South Gate. If that is the case then people like my father was thinking that the Japanese troops would mass themselves to meet the onslaught of the forces, not in the north, but in the south. It was all wrong, because they did not enter by the south gate. Father has been careful throughout the Japanese occupation, He was entrusted by the fleeing government of President Quezon to take care of the documents, the personal revolvers of the Congressmen who left with President Quezon. All were entrusted to him at the Alcazar Club. That was the meeting place of Quezon and his cabinet members.

So we were occupying the house in front of UST. That was our property then. My uncle was in the corner of

P. Campa and España. My father, his only brother, was in the corner of Moret and España. Papa sold that property for a song, just to get out of the place. Thinking that this will be the place of carnage, he got himself a property in front of the Madrigal house in Paco. Don Vicente Madrigal cannot refuse him. My great paternal grandfather and Don Vicente were friends. So he brought us all there, only to find out that this was not the safest place, Why safest place? Because of the American internees who were inside UST. Papa did not think of that, it did not even cross his mind. That the Americans will never sacrifice their internees there. So we hied off to that place in Paco. He bought himself a lot of water supply, all of the things that he can bring inside that asbestos lime house, thinking he could make a go of it. But when the carnage began, the Japanese did not use ordinary weapons. They dropped incendiary bombs from the roof and threw incendiary bombs on the houses in the south district because they were all amassed there. That is why there was so much carnage in Malate and Ermita. Those who were there cannot escape because the machine guns are lined up in front of their doors while the incendiary bombs were dropping all over the place. I don't know how papa was able to bring out my stepmother and Fr. Martinez who is now a Jesuit priest. According to my stepmother, the whole place was burning. It was like hell. My stepmother would say, "You know what saved us? It is only the portrait of Porta Vaga under the arms of your father which he rolled because he broke the frame and rolled the Blessed Virgin under his arm and the berretta." You know they broke a hole through the wall and crept there one by one. My father wet all the mattresses and with that, they plunged into the fire. It was really fire. That's why Fr. Martinez, even have scars here because he was still a baby at that time. His whole face was burned, but I know another miracle from God, there was no plastic surgeon on hand. He did not die, and you know, you cannot see the scar anymore. Naturally, it was removed. I mean in the seminary, little by little, it disappeared.

That was how the carnage started. Most of those 100,000 that they were reckoning are from the south. And you know, the southern part of Manila is the residential place, where all the elite of Manila are gathered. In Ermita and in Malate. I was told by a very dear friend of mine, who was a doctor, an intern at that time, that the doctors from PGH were fighting hand-to-hand Japanese *Kempeitai*. They entered the PGH where my friend saw her boyfriend bayoneted by the Japanese. Another doctor was with her. They were both interns. She then hid inside a cabinet. After the soldiers left, she went out of the cabinet and tried to find out if he was still alive. He was already dead. She got the body and she had the presence of mind to store it in a big refrigerator of the PGH. So after the holocaust was over, when the parents came looking for their child, she was the one who guided them to their son.

I don't know how many weeks that was after. That is how the carnage of Manila took place. People were crossing the river by the way. From the south, people were trying to cross the Pasig because they were told the Americans were already in the south. And, according to my stepmother, what was painful was that the Makapilis, Filipinos like us, took even the eyeglass of my father, and he's as blind as a bat without that eyeglass. And the little fault that she had, you know, a simple woman like my stepmother, would think of bringing rice and a little salt for her baby. They got even that rice. She was pleading to the Makapilis not to take the rice because it's for her little boy. But they did not listen to her. They got the eyeglass, they got the salt, they got the rice, before they could be allowed to crossover. But because my father has lost his eyeglass, they cannot cross over anymore to Pasig. So they retreated again and walked again until they reached Sta. Ana turf where my father had stables with his cousin, Don Pepe Zulueta. If you know, he was the speaker. But more tragic was what happened to Tio Pepe's family. They were all bayoneted in front of him including his only son, his wife, and so with Quirino's wife, Mrs. Quirino Syquia. She was also bayoneted by the *Kempeitai* right in front of Don Elpidio. President Quirino happened to be the lawyer of our family. That's why we are very close and we know how Doña Alicia died. But thank God, Papa was able to wait until things quieted down in that stable. I was newly married then. Well, not exactly newly married. I was already married two years. During the Japanese occupation, if you are a good father, all that you have in mind is to marry off your daughter because you are afraid that they will be raped or whatever. So that it was really hurried marriage between families because my husband was the son of his best friend.

Malabon did not suffer very much. That was where the food supply of Manila used to come. And if you must know, most of the Bataan refugees found themselves going, crossing to Malabon and Navotas. All the guns that were being smuggled to the guerrillas were passing through Malabon and Navotas North Bay Boulevard. They were being shipped under the grass that was used to feed the fodder of the horses, mostly of the Japanese. Under that were guns. And the couriers are women. Because the women have, you know, we have all kinds of charms—to smile and beguile the Japanese sentries. Some of them were smuggled through *bayongs* of *kangkong*. I would say that if there was anything that I can remember of the Japanese occupation, it was a leveler of society. Because during the Japanese occupation, the very rich became very poor, and the very poor became comfortably rich. Pianos, grand pianos at that were being traded, barter system, because who would care for *Mickey Mouse* money? The farmers and the rural folks would just laugh at you if you try to buy their things with the *Mickey Mouse* money. They will not sell. So to beguile them for two *ganta* rice, you have to part with your grand piano. And how I cried when I saw my favorite sofa being traded for a cup of *monggo*. It was my favorite sofa since childhood. I used to sleep there during siesta. And when I saw them being carried I said "Why naman Papa?" because I was not yet married then, it was just the beginning of the occupation. But Manila was already suffering from a lack of food. And the only thing he said was "Never mind, I'll buy you, how many do you want? Six of that kind? After 6 months, MacArthur will be here already. He will return." Everybody was hoping for the Americans to come. That was what life was then. But the civilians did their share.

I remember somebody yesterday describing the shortwave radio. Do you know that it was under pain of death if they catch (you) with a shortwave radio? But do you know that there was even a truck that goes around the streets of leading provinces and Manila? They said that it was like radar, Japanese instruments that pick up the sound of the radio, and it can trace where the short¬wave radio was being broadcasted. But you know what the flexible Filipino managed to do? I know this, I remember my father before I got married. It became the job of my husband after we got married. They used to remove a bulb and put another bulb, I think, or something. Well, the women were to go to the windows or downstairs and smile at passersby. While the men folks, at night at 8:00, would come and they would listen, huddled there to the Voice of America. Then this was recorded in shorthand and passed on from hand-to-hand. Much of this chore was done by the National Federation of Women's Clubs and the YMCA. At night, when everybody is asleep, they would be as quiet as little mice, and they would be muffling their typewriters and their mimeo graphic machines, and using only small candles. And with something to cover the light so that everything is dark around. Then in the morning, who fixed this up at 3 o'clock in the morning? Little boys in bicycles, 10, 11, 12 year-old boys circulate this and bring it to the doorsteps of people. They are called runners or couriers. This was how communication was done. And this was how the civilians helped the resistance movement. But it was terrible. Because the guerrilla themselves were not united. There was HUKBALAHAP quarreling with the USAFFE. That's normal because their ideologies are different.

But for these other guerrilla troops like PQOG quarelling with the Markings, with USAFFEs quarreling with President Quezon's Own Guerrilla. It's really senseless. If my husband gives a donation to the USAFFE, he will also have to give the others. You cannot just single out one group because you will disappear. Do you know that young as I was, I was married at 19, I was heavy with my child, I had to walk across the field to follow my husband, picked up by guerrilla units. I found out later it was the HUKBALAHAP because they discovered that he was supplying food to the USAFFE. But God will not abandon his people. I remember that midnight when I followed him, I told our *Kasamas*, what happened in Bulacan because our fishponds were in Bulacan. We had to keep the food rolling to the guerrillas because they needed the food supply. So, we had to man the fishpond and you cannot trust anybody except people of your blood and kin because, in those days, it was a dog-eat-dog system.

So we had to stay there. And I remember that I had to tell our *Kasamas* that if they did not accompany me, I will walk alone, I will try to look for where they brought my husband. And its good when I arrived at the camp of the HUKBALAHAP, the lady who appeared in the window after I said "Magandang Gabi po," it was 2:00 in the morning, "Ay, ang Ka Gloria, hoy, ang Ka Gloria ito, ito yung nagbibigay ng hipon sa amin. Ito ang nagpapakain sa anak mo. Uy, anong ginawa mo sa asawa nito, hah. Kaya pala pumunta rito, dahil dun daw sa asawa niya, kinuha niyo." That saved the day, you know, little kindnesses like that will pay off. I went home with my husband intact. Then from that time on, you know my husband never scolded me for giving away all the fish and the shrimps that I can find. Because I used to get scolded. What does a 19-year old person fresh from Assumption know about marketing and selling fish and shrimps? So I would give away those things, not knowing that all of that means life line not only for ourselves, but for the guerrillas that were relying on us. And another thing, after that incident, do you know that after the Americans came, and the Americans and the USAFFE's were in power in Bulacan, they picked up again my beloved husband for feeding the HUKBALAHAPS. This time, the one who saved him was his *kumpadre*, Alejo Santos. I think you know General Alejo Santos. You know what he did to the ROTC, the young cadets who picked up my husband? He made them walk on their knees from the church of the town of Bulacan to our place in Sta. Ana. He said "Don't you know that this man that you nearly killed was the one supplying us with food." While we were in the mountains, in the hills, in the fishpond, wherever they could hide. Well, I was the one who was in tears, and I said, "Ay Alex, 'wag na, wag na. Kawawa naman, huwag mo naman ganyanin ang mga bata." Ay really, it was terrible. I cannot go back without being emotional in those days. And when my dearest friend, a guerrilla commander, Aurora dela Rosa, sister to three commander-in-chiefs of USAFFE forces, Aurora dela Rosa killed herself by firing a gun on her temple after the liberation of Meycauayan, which she headed just before the American troops came in.

That was it, I said, I'm not gonna talk about anything about the war. I will just shut it off from my head. When the nephew came to me and said "Tita, Tita Auring is already dead." "Why?" I said. "Hindi ba siya ang nag-liberate ng Meycauayan?" And here I am, I was waiting that we will be celebrating in great joy because the Americans were already going that way. He said, "We just don't know, she asked me to hoist the flag in the flagpole, she got her service pistol and fired the shot at her temple."

Up to now, I'm asking "Why Auring, why?" I do not know the answer. I always pray.

And finally, another heroic act of our women during those days, believe it or not, was to line themselves in the street whenever some prisoners are going to be brought by *Kempeitais*, especially during the Death March. They would be wearing voluminous skirts. And you know every time the Japanese soldiers would look to another direction, they would pull one of those soldiers, and hide him in their skirts, and that soldier will scamper like a little rabbit from one skirt to another. How many skirts he go under? I don't know. Until he could find his way out. Another act of heroism of our women, I would say. It takes courage to do that, while you are smuggling soldiers there under your skirt, you are smiling, graciously beguiling the Japanese. This thing that happened in EDSA I, when they placed flowers and the nuns met the tanks, that's not new to us. That's what we did for the Japanese soldiers also. We did that because we had another motive, that's to distract their attention. That's how guerrilla units were also formed. And finally you know these *bayongs*? They were very good places for hiding documents that we snatched from the military camps of the Japanese. Women used to act as secretaries to the generals of the Japanese forces. And when they hear of troops going to be moved, or rice to be brought in from, or rice to be shipped out. By the way, nobody mentioned yesterday the *sisid* rice. The *sisid* rice is the rice that they have to throw in to the water to save them from the Japanese soldiers because they are going to be shipped to Tokyo or somewhere where there is fighting going on. And then once it is quiet, our own divers would dive and go after those sacks of rice, bring them out to somewhere for drying then sell them as *sisid* rice. Thank you.

POSTSCRIPT

Just to make you laugh, do you know that one of the funniest things I remember were barrio women selling in the markets dressed up in the elegant gowns that used to grace Manila Hotel. Because that was acquired by barter, you know, well there was no place to wear them, so they wore them to market.

The Presenters

FR. MIGUEL BERNAD, S.J.

Born on 8 May 1917 in Ozamiz City, he entered the Society of Jesus in 1932 at the Jesuit Novitiate and was ordained as a priest in 1946. He studied Theology at Woodstock College in Maryland and graduated magna cum laude. He finished his master's and doctorate degrees at Yale University, wrote numerous books about Philippine history and culture, and taught at several universities.

JOSE ANTONIO CUSTODIO

A graduate of B.A. and M.A. in History from the University of the Philippines, he has written several historical essays in various leading newspapers, as well as journals of the Armed Forces of the Philippines. He was consultant on national security and defense, the curator of the AFP Museum, and he taught history at the University of Asia and the Pacific.

DR. AUGUSTO V. DE VIANA

A Ph.D. graduate of the University of Santo Tomas (Magna Cum Laude), he has written several books about history. He was the former head of the Research, Publications, and Heraldry Division of the National Historical Institute, now NHCP.

DR. LUIS C. DERY

A graduate of B.S. and M.A. (Teaching) and Ph.D. (History) from the University of the Philippines, he has written several books, essays, and articles on history and culture. He was a professor of history and an active member of historical and cultural associations.

PROF. JOSE MA. BONIFACIO ESCODA

A graduate of Adamson University (A.B. History), he also taught Spanish literature and grammar, History, Philosophy, Sociology, and Psychology at his alma mater. He also contributes articles to newspapers.

DR. ARMAND V. FABELLA

He obtained his A.B. Economics degree (Cum Laude) at Harvard College in 1951 and was awarded the TOYM in 1962. He was Secretary of the Department of Education, Culture and Sports from 1992–1994 and he also authored several books and articles on economics and education.

DR. RICARDO T. JOSE

A Ph.D. graduate of Tokyo University of Foreign Studies, he was an Outstanding Young Scientist awardee and has written numerous books, pamphlets, and articles on history and culture, as well as historical television documentaries.

F. SIONIL JOSE

Born on 3 December 1929 in Rosales, Pangasinan, he had written a number of novels, short stories, and essays. He was awarded the Ramon Magsaysay Award in 1980 and the National Artist Award in 2001. He was the founder of the publishing firm Solidaridad.

EDGAR KROHN, JR.

Born on 23 September 1928 in Manila, he was in high school when the Japanese conquered Manila. He was a founding member of the Petroleum Association of the Philippines and a member of the Rotary Club of Makati and Memorare Manila 1945 Foundation, Inc.

DR. BENITO J. LEGARDA, JR.

He had a Bachelor of Science degree in Social Sciences (Magna Cum Laude) from Georgetown University and M.A. and Ph.D. in Economics from Harvard University. He taught at FEATI, Far Eastern University, and Ateneo de Manila, published numerous articles on history and economics, and held important positions in government and civic organizations.

OSCAR M. LOPEZ

Born on 19 April 1930, he studied at Harvard College and graduated cum laude (Bachelor of Arts) in 1951. He was the Chairman and Chief Executive Officer concurrently of First Philippine Holdings Corporation.

COL. CESAR P. POBRE

He was a retired colonel of the Philippine Armed Forces, a consultant/senior researcher fellow at the Office of Strategic and Special Studies, and a lecturer at the Command and General Staff Colleges of the AFP. A graduate of the Philippine Military Academy, he took his M.A. in History at the University of the Philippines. He had also written a number of books.

FR. JAMES B. REUTER, S.J.

He came to the Philippines in 1938 and was interned by the Japanese at Los Baños, Laguna during the war. He was the recipient of several awards, including the Ramon Magsaysay Award for journalism and communication in 1989.

GLORIA M. SANTOS

She was Dean of External Relations at St. Mary's College in Quezon City. She had a BSE degree and an M.A. in History from the University of the Philippines, an M.A. in education from the Far Eastern University, and a Ph.D. in theology from the Dorset Institute of Higher

Education in England. She was a regular lecturer of the Philippine Historical Association.